D1807292

Between Foreign and Family

Asian American Studies Today

This series publishes scholarship on cutting-edge themes and issues, including broadly based histories of both long-standing and more recent immigrant populations; focused investigations of ethnic enclaves and understudied subgroups; and examinations of relationships among various cultural, regional, and socioeconomic communities. Of particular interest are subject areas in need of further critical inquiry, including transnationalism, globalization, homeland polity, and other pertinent topics.

Series Editor: Huping Ling, Truman State University

Chien-Juh Gu, *The Resilient Self: Gender, Immigration, and Taiwanese Americans*

Stephanie Hinnershitz, *Race, Religion, and Civil Rights: Asian Students on the West Coast, 1900–1968*

Jennifer Ann Ho, *Racial Ambiguity in Asian American Culture*

Helene K. Lee, *Between Foreign and Family: Return Migration and Identity Construction among Korean Americans and Korean Chinese*

Haiming Liu, *From Canton Restaurant to Panda Express: A History of Chinese Food in the United States*

Jun Okada, *Making Asian American Film and Video: History, Institutions, Movements*

Kim Park Nelson, *Invisible Asians: Korean American Adoptees, Asian American Experiences and Racial Exceptionalism*

Zelideth María Rivas and Debbie Lee-DiStefano, eds., *Imagining Asia in the Americas*

David S. Roh, Betsy Huang, and Greta A. Niu, eds., *Techno-Orientalism: Imagining Asia in Speculative Fiction, History, and Media*

Jane H. Yamashiro, *Constructing Japanese American Identity in Japan: Transnationalism, Diaspora, and Ancestral Homeland Migration*

Between Foreign and Family

Return Migration and Identity Construction among Korean Americans and Korean Chinese

HELENE K. LEE

Rutgers University Press

New Brunswick, Newark, and Camden, New Jersey and London

978-0-8135-8614-4
978-0-8135-8613-7
978-0-8135-8615-1

Cataloging-in-Publication data is available from the Library of Congress.

A British Cataloging-in-Publication record for
this book is available from the British Library.

www.rutgersuniversitypress.org

Manufactured in the United States of America

For my mother, Hae Soon Lee, and my father, Hee Young Lee,
and Aurora Han Byeol Lee

Contents

Between Foreign and Family

Introduction

On a warm fall evening, Song Lim—a young, third-generation Korean Chinese man—and I meet in *Hongdae*, a vibrant neighborhood near Hongik University.[1] We pass Starbucks, Pizza Hut, *naengmyeon* noodle shops, and *odeng* bars to get to our destination, a newly opened TGI Fridays restaurant. As we walk in, I feel as though I have been transported back to the United States by the restaurant's decor and booths, down to the button-adorned red-and-white-striped uniform of our server. Song Lim pores over the laminated menu filled with unfamiliar dishes, asking me lots of questions and ultimately settling on an order of nachos. Song Lim is excited, though in the end, a little disappointed by its blandness. Like the other students who attend the weekly English class I offer at a Korean Chinese church, Song Lim only uses formal Korean to address me, often prefacing my name with *seonsaeng*, the honorific title of "teacher," though this does not stop him from making me the target of good-natured ribbing. After dinner, he insists on following the South Korean social convention of multiple stages, or *cha*, that requires changing venues for each round of drinks or meals with no fewer than four stops.[2] We wander into different bars and cafes for the next few hours, and what strikes me is how situations I take for granted in these neighborhoods frequented by American tourists or expatriots are new for Song Lim. He repeatedly remarks on the novelty of ordering from a nearly all-English menu and drinking in places filled with loud conversations in English. He has lived in Seoul for several years but has never ventured into Hongdae, *Sinchon*, or *Itaewon*—areas where most of the Korean Americans in my study reside and/or frequent. Likewise, I have not gone to parts of the city where he spends most of his time.

Song Lim and I are part of the growing foreign population in South Korea, which is estimated at over 3 percent.[3] Foreigners, particularly return migrants, challenge a national myth that equates ethnicity, nationality, and race as nearly synonymous concepts. While Song Lim and I talk to each other in Korean, an astute eavesdropper might note our "foreign" accents and that his is different from mine. It is a second language for both of us, though Song Lim's skills far exceed my own—as he is quick to point out. Constantly. We are both ethnic Koreans who were born and raised abroad; he as a third-generation Korean Chinese and me as a second-generation Korean American. Yet on every level, the difference between his experiences in Seoul and mine is wide. The gap begins with the ways we grew up—in China and the United States, respectively—and how we understood what it meant to be Korean in that context. We entered South Korea on different visas, which had a profound impact on our mobility, our legal status, and the kinds of jobs we performed. We are also treated and perceived by South Koreans very differently even though we are both members of the Korean diaspora.

I choose to begin with my night out with Song Lim for a number of reasons. He humanizes the stereotyped image of an undocumented migrant. He does not hide in the shadows, constantly surveilling his environment out of a fear of deportation, although he is certainly on guard against that possibility. He is social and easygoing, and looks and acts like many other young straight men his age. Song Lim occasionally goes out on dates with South Korean and Korean Chinese women and shares many entertaining stories about his successes and failures in that department. Song Lim enjoys evenings out with his friends—mostly other Korean Chinese labor migrants who have worked on construction sites with him. Interestingly, other than the time he spends with me, Song Lim says he has had no contact with Korean Americans in Seoul. But like other Korean Chinese in the study, he is very aware of the differences between his social location and those of Korean Americans, Korean Japanese, and other return migrants from "more developed" countries.

In contrast, the Korean Americans with whom I speak make little mention of other return migrants in Seoul, and most are likely unaware of the discrimination that Korean Chinese like Song Lim face every day. Our evening in Hongdae speaks to the presence of unmarked yet unmistakable spaces—what I call "geo-ethnic bubbles"—within which certain kinds of immigrants are concentrated and "outsiders" rarely transgress.[4] How is it that Korean Chinese like Song Lim and Korean Americans like myself occupy very different areas of Seoul and have social networks that almost always exclude each other's communities? What constitutes these distinct Korean American and Korean Chinese "bubbles," and why don't they overlap or interact?

This book takes up these and other questions by centering on why Korean Americans and Korean Chinese "return" to Seoul despite being shaped by very different national contexts and having little previous engagement with the ancestral homeland. What do they hope to find that they can't find in their country of citizenship, where they were born and/or raised for most, if not all, of their lives? What do they experience once they arrive? Beyond an imagined homecoming or a search for roots, what do they learn about Korean identity from living in Seoul?

I use the terms "return migrant" and "return migration" while acknowledging their problematic nature. Strictly speaking, only the first generation would be considered "immigrants." Second and later generations are not necessarily "migrants" because they have been born and/or raised for most, if not all, of their lives in their country of citizenship. Likewise, the idea of a "homeland" is also complicated for the second and later generations, who might be "returning" to a place they have never been and might consider multiple nation-states to be "home." Anthropologists Anastasia Christou and Russell King note the proliferation of terms used in return migration research that emphasize various aspects of this kind of migration, including but not limited to "ancestral return," "ethnic return," "heritage migrants," "roots migration," "reverse migration," and their own term, "counter-diaspora."[5] I use "return migrant" in this book because of the respondents' own framing of their migration to South Korea as a "return home." Additionally, many identify strongly as immigrants, as having lived lives that have always been in motion and connected to more than one nation simultaneously, because of their family histories.

Making Meanings of Koreanness

Central to these return migration projects are the multiple meanings ascribed to "Koreanness." Linguist Ferdinand de Saussure uses the notion of "signs" as a way through which people "make meaning" to organize the world around them. In his model, the "signifier" is the "form" that the sign takes, the "signified" refers to the concept it represents, and "signification" represents the linking of the "signifier" with the "signified."[6] Importantly, the relationship between the signifier and signified is created and interpreted by people themselves, and everyone within a given system must be in agreement about what a sign is signifying. To use "cat" as a simple example, people who hear or see the word "cat" must have an agreed upon concept of a cat that distinguishes it from a dog, mouse, or another animal that might share similar characteristics with it (e.g., four-legged, furry) but is not a cat.

But what happens when the relationship between the signifier and signified is deeply contested, as is the case when "race" is the signifier in question?[7] In the United States, there is much debate over "race" itself, including the central question of whether "race" actually exists or whether it comes into being only because of the meanings attached to markers like skin color, hair texture, and nation of origin. Are race and racial identity biologically or socially determined? Some point to the election of the first Black president of the United States as evidence that we live in a "postracial" moment where race no longer constrains our economic, political, and social realities. Others cite data ranging from the disproportionate incarceration rates of communities of color, to longstanding patterns of residential segregation in major urban cities and disparate educational outcomes between White and non-White students as evidence that race and *racism* has actually deepened in significance. Comparative race studies confound these discussions further because the analysis requires signification within multiple national contexts. Micol Seigel notes, "If there is no exact equation between sign and signified in one place, there is even less hope for perfect equivalence when trying to reconcile two—or more, if the people involved speak different languages, and more again if the observer stands at another historical vantage point, since racial schemas change over time even in a single place."[8]

In this book, I apply Seigel's discussion of race to a comparative analysis of competing meanings of ethnicity in the context of return migration. While the homeland can serve an important purpose for members of a diaspora, less is known about the *comparative* dimensions of transnationalism when *multiple* diasporic communities return to the homeland with foreign citizenship, varying levels of cultural and linguistic fluency, and differing ideas about what their ethnic identity means to them. For the Korean American and Korean Chinese return migrants in this study, "Koreanness" operates as both a cultural construct and an inherited trait as well as shorthand for the contested components of their class, ethnic, and national identities in both their nations of origin and the ethnic homeland. It signifies something deeply personal, nourished in the home and by their families, and performed daily through the food they eat, the language(s) they speak, and the customs and traditions they perform. Koreanness, at times, can be a liability, particularly when it comes to experiences with marginalization in China and the United States. At other times, Koreanness can be an asset, the source of something immutable that does not fade over generations and creates a sense of community and connection back to the country from which their parents and/or grandparents emigrated. It informs the decisions made by these return migrants, including a choice, motivated in equal measure by economics and emotion, to move abroad to South Korea.

Drawing on ethnographic observations and interview data with Korean Americans and Korean Chinese in Seoul, I highlight what I call "logics of transnationalism" to show how these actors make meaning of the intersecting dimensions of Koreanness—racial, emotional, economic, gendered, and historical. By logics, I refer to the ways in which concepts like "citizenship," "blood," "family," and "culture" feature prominently in the stories return migrants tell and circulate among each other that give substance to what it means to be Korean in this particular historical moment. Returns to the homeland require interactions with South Korean institutions and individuals, which force return migrants to confront their homeland as more than an idealized, romanticized place. While Korean Chinese and Korean Americans both meet the fundamental criteria for ethnic membership as defined by blood and ancestry, the ascribed value of their kind of Koreanness reflects the demands of the global economy as well as the goals of South Korea's ongoing globalization project. By moving to South Korea, return migrants are subject to inconsistent and arbitrary "rules" of ethnic inclusion and exclusion that challenge their claims to Koreanness. Claiming Koreanness is not purely personal; it is also embedded in institutional and collective dynamics. Logics reveal the contested, multilayered process of ethnic and national identity construction in which the South Korean state, employers, workers, family members, friends, and lovers all have a stake.

Return Migration and the Significance of Ethnicity in a Transnational World

The theoretical work of Nina Glick Schiller, Linda Basch, and Cristina Blanc-Szanton made an important intervention on research in the fields of immigration and racial and ethnic studies.[9] This transnational approach calls for greater engagement with the messiness of lives that are based on ties to more than one nation simultaneously. An examination of return migration projects extends our understandings of transnationalism because diasporic actors must shift from an "imagined community" with whom they have little to no direct contact based on ancestral ties and an invented shared history to a "knowable community" of coworkers, relatives, and friends they interact with on a day-to-day level who may directly challenge their claims for inclusion.[10] Transnationalism is not an abstract condition. It is shaped by social, economic, and political forces and maintained by practices both broad and narrow, individual and institutional, transitory and enduring.

Return migrations challenge the predictions of migration scholars. Earlier migrations were assumed to be one-way and permanent, especially when the flow was from peripheral, developing, or underdeveloped nations to core, postindustrialized nations (often in the West). In the traditional model, (im)migrants, compelled by "push" factors such as poverty, few economic opportunities, or political persecution, arrive in a country in which they are linguistically, culturally, and, in some cases, racially and/or ethnically foreign to the majority population. Once they arrive in their "host" nation, immigrants put down roots and cut ties with their country of origin, looking ahead to the future rather than the past. Most carry little expectation of immediate acceptance and anticipate facing resistance or even hostility to their presence.

Return migration differs from conventional migratory flows because of the simultaneous yet contradictory sensation of familiarity and foreignness that comes with coethnicity. Return migrants often have a strong emotional and physical connection to a country they identify as their ethnic homeland and often anticipate unquestioned recognition by homeland ethnics as "family." Contrary to expectations, social scientists have found that when members of a diaspora "return," they are more likely to reevaluate rather than strengthen their attachments to their ancestral homeland and their ethnic identities more broadly.[11]

Previous ethnographic research on return migration has focused primarily on a single diasporic community.[12] Other work narrowly centers on the search for belonging and roots through short-term heritage trips or relatively short family visits.[13] The analysis has centered on a single axis—nationality—undertheorizing how additional axes of dissimilarity such as gender, emigration histories, and generational status work across and within multiple diasporic communities. This book's comparative analysis sheds light on the ways asymmetrical relationships between nation-states are played out through the bodies of return migrants. I trace where the logics of Korean Americans and Korean Chinese intersect and where they diverge as a result of the hierarchical differences in diaspora–homeland relationships that have been flattened in the uniform, singular characterization found in previous studies on diaspora.

Transformations in Contemporary South Korea

South Korea provides an interesting case study because of its dramatic economic and political changes over the past sixty years. Shedding its past as the "Hermit Kingdom," South Korea has shifted from a migrant-sending to a migrant-receiving country as one of four newly industrialized countries often referred to as "Asian Tigers." Rising standards of living and a growing demand for necessary skills in a globalizing economy has led to an increase in migrants from both developing and postindustrialized countries alike. As a result, South Korea is forced to balance the constant demand for cheaper labor with the social problems associated with an increasing presence of foreign migrant workers. Beginning in the 1980s and continuing through to the present, Korean Chinese and Korean Americans constitute two of the largest communities of coethnic foreign workers in South Korea. As such, they are ideal subjects to understand the ways the South Korean state strategically recruits coethnic workers to provide necessary labor without extending the boundaries of nationhood and citizenship.

The focus on return migration to South Korea offers additional insights into comparative race relations when different racial logics operating in three national contexts—South Korea, the United States, and China—collide. After migrants arrive, how and why do their receptions by South Koreans differ so dramatically in a national context in which ideas of race, ethnicity, and nation are nearly synonymous? Korean Chinese and Korean Americans returning to an "imagined" homeland must grapple with the *relational* aspect of ethnic identity when it intersects with ideas about nationality, citizenship, emigration histories, gender, family, blood, and ancestry in a specific national context. Meanings of Koreanness are negotiated within China and the United States, respectively, but then reshaped in encounters in South Korea. In that sense, their ethnic identities are shaped by the larger political and economic relationships transpiring between China, the United States, and South Korea. Additionally, with the division of the Korean peninsula into two separate nation-states, Koreanness is negotiated across not only multiple homes but also multiple homelands, and this has consequences for diasporic Korean communities.

The stories in this book reveal the intimacies of home and Koreanness in the lives of return migrants. For one reason or another, the Korean Americans and Korean Chinese in this book have settled in Seoul to claim a part of the homeland for themselves. They use stories from their past and ideas about blood, customs, and traditions from their families to legitimize their connection to South Korea. Returns force encounters between Koreans who never left the Korean peninsula and the descendants of those who did. They also force a rethinking of relationships and responsibilities—between nations and citizens, homelands and diasporas, parents and children, women and men, husbands and wives, girlfriends and boyfriends, employers and employees, and between two communities within the same diaspora.

This research is based on ethnographic data and interviews with 64 diasporic Korean return migrants from China and the United States over sixteen months of fieldwork in the Seoul metropolitan area. A more detailed methodological discussion and tables with key characteristics for respondents are included in the appendix. Thirty-three interviews were conducted with Korean Chinese: 18 women and 15 men, mostly second- and third-generation ethnic Koreans. Thirty-one interviews were with Korean Americans:

18 women and 13 men, all of whom identified as 1.5- or second-generation ethnic Koreans. While this does not constitute a representative sample, the consistency of their responses about life in Seoul suggests widely held attitudes in South Korea toward Korean Chinese and Korean Americans and vice versa. Respondents all reside in Seoul, a top destination for migrants as the cultural, political, and economic center of South Korea. All names have been changed to protect the privacy of respondents, Anglicized or Koreanized pseudonyms preserve the original given names. I present their stories in this book as accurately as possible to respect their importance to respondents as part of their individual narratives as immigrants while also contextualizing them as part of broader contestations over Koreanness imbedded in current geopolitics and South Korea's own globalization project.

Organization of the Book

Each chapter centers on a particular dimension of transnationalism—national, emotional, economic, gendered, and historical—and analyzes the interlocking and, occasionally, conflicting sets of logics that bridge the gap between expectation and reality in the lives of these return migrants.

Chapter 1 focuses on the "premigration condition," built on *economic* and *emotional logics*, that impels some Korean Chinese and Korean Americans to return to their ancestral homeland. Born and/or raised as children and grandchildren of Korean immigrants in two countries that espouse commitments to cultural pluralism among its citizenry, Korean Americans and Korean Chinese are told that their ethnic identities are not an impediment to full belonging—to be Chinese or American is to respect and protect difference. Yet for Korean Americans, *racial logics* in the United States result in feelings of marginalization because of the ways white privilege is embedded and sustained by institutions and interactions. A "true" American is understood to be ethnically neutral and racially White. For Korean Chinese, the comparatively small numbers of ethnic Koreans in a population of over one billion that is overwhelming ethnic Han translates into similar feelings of marginalization. Despite the fact that, in the majority of cases, their parents and grandparents largely framed their emigration from the Korean peninsula for better social and economic opportunities, these Korean Americans and Korean Chinese choose decades later to move back to South Korea. This chapter ends with a discussion of the motivations for their return migration.

Chapter 2 explores the *economics* of transnationalism as Korean Chinese and Korean Americans negotiate the South Korean visa system and labor market. Access to more privileged visa categories depends on the abilities of coethnic return migrants to prove their ties to the *South Korean* nation, thus making them "family" in the eyes of the State. Likewise, their particular set of skills is assessed in terms of their economic value to South Koreans. For Korean Chinese, their linguistic fluency and cultural knowledge of Korean traditions and customs and willingness to do manual labor eschewed by middle-class, educated South Koreans make them ideal workers in 3-D (dirty, dangerous, and difficult) and service industries. As a result, Korean Chinese become vulnerable to exploitation in low-waged, temporary, and unstable jobs. On the other hand, Korean Americans—with their US citizenship, cultural capital, and native English skills, combined with college and graduate degrees from elite colleges and universities—can access higher-paid, higher-status jobs, particularly in the industries of English-language teaching and business. This chapter provides an ethnographic account of how the *affective* logics rooted in the discourse of family intersect with the *economic* weight assigned to Koreanness in the South Korean labor market.

Chapter 3 centers on the *gendered* logics of Koreanness within the social lives of Korean Americans that are expressed through the language of culture and morality. I trace how notions of "authentic" femininities and hybridized masculinities create a "totem pole" made visible in their social lives that integrate national, racial, and gender ideologies. Korean American "kings" find themselves positioned near the top, while Korean American women find themselves, in the words of one respondent, "lower than lepers," at the bottom of the social hierarchy. This framework rests on the simultaneous emasculation and marginalization of Asian American men and exoticization and hypersexualization of Asian American women. The move to South Korea allows Korean American men to experience social desirability as a result of the privileges of their US cultural capital, while Korean American women are criticized for their lack of authenticity as Korean women.

Chapter 4 focuses on the historical dimensions of transnational identity for Korean Chinese, also known as *Joseonjok*—literally "the people of *Joseon*." I trace how Korean Chinese use a set of *historical* logics that link authentic Koreanness to Joseon—the last and longest ruling dynasty when Confucian values and doctrines were integrated into Korean society, and modern Korean language and cultural norms were established. At a time when Korean Americans and Korean Japanese have access to more generous visa categories and North Korean refugees are eligible for South Korean citizenship and government subsidies, Korean Chinese recast their identities as the "original" and "true" Koreans as a strategy to offset the structural disadvantages they face in their everyday lives in Seoul, where they are largely seen as dirty, uneducated, poor, and a potential "social problem."

Chapter 5 explores how the logics of cosmopolitan Koreanness and the notion of global citizenship enable Korean Americans and Korean Chinese to focus on the positive benefits that they feel outweigh the challenges they face during their return migration projects. "Cosmopolitan Koreanness" becomes a way to think of themselves as "better Koreans" than South Koreans *and* "better Americans" and "better Chinese" than the dominant ethnic and racial majority in their countries of citizenship. In many ways, their experiences in Seoul, both positive and negative, enable Korean Chinese and Korean Americans to accrue the greatest social and economic benefits while in South Korea and a better future once they eventually return to the China and the United States, respectively.

Ultimately, through return migration, Korean Americans and Korean Chinese learn about the "illogics" of Koreanness. Korean Americans are largely penalized for their cultural deficits and for being "too American," as evidenced by the fact that they cannot talk, act, or look like South Koreans. At the same time, Korean Chinese, who actually possess the cultural and linguistic fluency that Korean Americans lack, are summarily dismissed because their cultural capital is perceived as outdated within contemporary South Korea. They are additionally handicapped by the absence of formal ties to either South or North Korea. Multiple claims of Koreanness call into question who is—and, more important, who is not—Korean. At issue for the Korean Americans and Korean Chinese in this study are the very meanings of "Koreanness" in the changing context of postindustrialized South Korea. In short, being Korean matters, but not in the same way for all groups. This book is about the power of the multiple logics of transnationalism in shaping how return migrants think and talk about Koreanness, the concrete impact it has on their lives in Seoul, and what they see as the future of Koreanness once they return to their country of citizenship.

1

The Premigration Condition

My grandfather—my father too—they never talked to me about South Korea. I never thought about South Korea and what things are like there. I grew up in China; my citizenship is Chinese. But after living here [in Seoul] for eight years, I have come to learn things that I didn't know before. . . . I realize that my blood *is* Korean. I heard Korean inside my house, my grandparents *are* Korean [italics indicate her emphasis]. Here [South Korea] is where my roots are. I realize now that my birth country is not where my roots are.

With these words, Hee Sook, a Korean Chinese graduate student, describes the changes in her relationship to her Korean and Chinese identities because of her return to South Korea. She begins with the language of citizenship and the fact that she has lived in China her whole life. But Koreanness is framed as something encoded in her DNA and a fundamental part of who she is despite her Chinese citizenship. Her Koreanness—as signified by her blood, ancestry, and cultural knowledge—becomes more salient the longer she is in South Korea. Even as a third-generation Korean Chinese, she comes to see her true roots as originating from somewhere in the Korean peninsula rather than the country where she was born.

Her experience is evidence that ethnic attachments to an ancestral homeland remain significant past the immigrant generation and can intensify as a result of "returns." As "perpetual foreigners," in their countries of citizenship, individuals like Hee Sook are reminded that their ethnic identities are a fundamental, unchangeable aspect of who they are and how they are perceived. Narratives of emigration passed down by parents and grandparents sustain connections between diasporic communities and the homeland over generations, even if they are rooted in romanticized or idealized memories rather than direct contact.

In this chapter, I highlight the competing logics of citizenship and blood within the "premigration condition" that marks South Korea as a "homeland" for return migrants and through which "Koreanness" permeates the everyday lives of second- and later-generation Korean Americans and Korean Chinese. Beginning with the context of their differing emigration histories, I trace how Koreanness is *created* and *controlled* by national policies of diversity and multiculturalism in the United States and China, respectively. These institutional factors structure the entry, incorporation, and marginalization of immigrants and shape the ways Koreanness becomes the source of second-class citizenship marked by discrimination and racism. Finally, I show how "returns" become a way to *reclaim* South Korea as a "true" home.

Theories of Ethnicity

Returns run counter to prevailing theories of ethnicity, which hypothesize that, over time, second and later generations will gradually assimilate to the dominant culture in their countries of settlement.[1] Social science research on ethnicity within immigrant groups, particularly in the US context, has been highly influenced by "straight line" paradigms such as the "race relation cycle" advanced by Robert Park, a sociologist associated with the Chicago school.[2] These assimilation frameworks assume a one-directional migration flow in which immigrants cut ties to their nations of origin and gradually become absorbed into the "melting pot" of American society. However, these theories have largely been critiqued for their focus on the experiences of early European immigrants. Furthermore, early African migrants were brought explicitly under an economic and political system of slavery that erased their humanity, leaving no possibility for full incorporation or assimilation in American society. Assimilation theories also inadequately address the experiences of the growing numbers of migrants from Latin America, the Caribbean, Asia, and Africa after 1965 that fundamentally transformed mainstream "American" culture.

Traditional frameworks fail to account for the ways racism and discrimination at both the institutional and interpersonal levels can make ethnic actors feel like they are not "authentic" national subjects in home countries with official policies that espouse cultural pluralism. Newer theories of segmented assimilation argue for more "bumpy than straight" frameworks that consider the different range of challenges ethnic groups might encounter due to US racial logics, class status, and religious identities. Some argue that even as housing, social networks, marriage, and dating patterns become more integrated, ethnic identities remain salient even into the third and fourth generation.[3] This is facilitated through what Philip Kasinitz calls "ethnic replenishment," which is provided by later-generation ethnics who sustain ties to both their "home" countries of citizenship and ancestral ethnic "homeland" countries.[4]

However, meanings of ethnicity are dynamic and change over time. One reason for this might be that individuals beyond the initial immigrant generation can voluntarily "opt into" an ethnic identity using specific markers as meaningful symbols of ethnic affiliation in ways that do not require sustained amounts of time and energy and can be adapted to fit easily within one's existing lifestyle.[5] These invented traditions and cultures might be unrecognizable to newer immigrants or contemporary residents in homeland countries but retain significance among later-generation ethnic Americans who have little to no substantive direct ties to the "old country."

While most second- and later-generation individuals do not choose to uproot their lives to return to their family's country of origin, those who do physically return for medium- to long-term migration projects provide insight into the economic, social, and emotional factors that contribute to this particular transnational practice. A close examination of the premigration condition broadens our understandings of how Koreanness becomes imbedded within everyday practices and decision-making processes. It also helps prevent "ethnic drift" in the face of assimilation pressures, long-term separation from the homeland, and the gradual loss of language skills and cultural traditions.[6] A nuanced understanding of the ways Koreanness is constructed by Korean Americans in the United States and Korean Chinese in China provides an essential foundation to contextualize their experiences in South Korea.

Creating Koreanness through Emigration Histories

Meanings of Koreanness for Korean Americans and Korean Chinese in my study begin with the emigration histories of their parents and grandparents. The stories of why their families left mention a range of external factors including famine, military conflict, occupation by foreign powers, underdevelopment, general lack of economic opportunities and political repression. Once these emigrants settled abroad, their Koreanness had to be reconstructed within a new national framework in which ethnicity and nationality were no longer tightly intertwined. In the next section, I provide a brief discussion of the historical contexts for the establishment of ethnic Korean immigrant communities in China and the United States to highlight the key differences and similarities between the two.

The Qing government loosened restrictions for China's northeast border with the Korean peninsula in 1881. Many ethnic Koreans took advantage of this new pathway to flee deteriorating economic conditions and a severe famine. A second wave of migrants was spurred by the annexation of the Korean peninsula by Japan in 1910 and the political repression that followed. As a result, the number of Koreans in the area known as Manchuria (near present-day North Korea and Russia) rose from ten thousand to over one million.[7] Using historical claims that parts of Manchuria originally belonged to the Korean kingdom under the Koguryo Dynasty and were now part of the Japanese empire, Japanese troops began an aggressive advance in northeastern China. This further increased tensions in the region. Historians note that Koreans in China during this period played pivotal roles in the resistance movement against the Japanese during the Chinese People's Liberation War, were highly active in the Chinese Communist Party, and were instrumental in the founding of the new socialist People's Republic of China in 1949.[8]

With the establishment of formal North and South Korean governments in 1948, most ethnic Koreans in China became exiled, no longer able to return "home" to the dismantled kingdom of Joseon. With few new immigrants from North and South Korea to China, Korean Chinese communities stabilized under generally favorable state policies toward minorities in China, maintaining "dual identities" as Chinese citizens with a strong sense of Korean identity.[9] Based on Chinese national census data, an estimated 1.8 million Koreans currently live in China, making them the eleventh-largest minority group and one of the largest Korean diasporic communities living outside of the peninsula.[10] Korean Chinese remain concentrated in three provinces in Northeast China: Jilin, Heilongjiang, and Liaoning.[11] Presently, approximately 40 percent of the Korean Chinese population resides in Yanbian Korean Autonomous Prefecture in Jilin Province, which was formally established in 1955. This concentration was reflected among the Korean Chinese respondents in this study, over half of whom came from hometowns in Yanbian.

While much of the migrant flow from the Korean peninsula to China occurred between 1880 and 1948, emigration to the United States occurred much later, through three channels: migrant labor, military families, and international adoptions. A small number of Korean immigrants arrived in Hawai'i as plantation laborers in the early twentieth century. In addition, some Korean women arrived in the United States following the Korean War as part of the War Brides Act of 1945 alongside their American GI husbands. Over the past seventy years, since the end of the Second World War and the Korean War, the US military has stationed nearly 30,000 troops in fifteen bases across South Korea. As a result, military families have always played a key role in the demographics of contemporary Korean American communities. Early military wives sponsored family members in South Korea, triggering a small wave of early Korean immigration. International adoptions from South Korea also rose exponentially following the end of the Korean War. Based on annual reports/yearbooks of immigration, South Korea was the largest "source country" for international adoptions between 1976 and 1985.[12] Anthropologist Eleana Kim estimates organizations such as Holt International Children's Services facilitated the international adoptions of more than one hundred thousand Korean children between 1953 and 2008.[13] However, the overall numbers of Korean immigrants were relatively low until the passage of the Immigration and Nationality Act of 1965, also known as the Hart-Cellar Act.

After 1965, US immigration policies prioritized skilled-labor recruitment and family reunification, which opened new avenues for Korean immigrants. In what has been referred to as the "brain drain," core countries like the United States actively sought professional, highly educated individuals from newly industrialized countries like South Korea to fill gaps in the domestic labor market. Edward Park and John Park point to the creation of H-1B visas, designed for college-educated professionals with highly skilled degrees, as an example of how US policies explicitly molded the makeup of contemporary Asian American communities.[14] Immigrants from Asia—including South Korea, the Philippines, India, Japan, and China—were, and continue to be, heavily recruited in the fields of information technology, engineering, education, and health care and constitute nearly 75 percent of the beneficiaries of these H-1B visas. Asian immigrant H-1B holders who came to the United States as part of this initiative were highly educated, urban, middle-class citizens in their home countries with the resources and skills to immigrate. Many parents of the Korean American respondents in this study arrived after 1965 as highly skilled professionals or educational migrants seeking advanced degrees.

Korean immigration to the United States increased steadily, and South Korea became the third-largest sending country behind Mexico and the Philippines in the period between 1976 and 1990.[15] Many Koreans were motivated by "push" factors such as economic underdevelopment, few employment options, political instability under successive military dictatorships between 1960 and 1987, and the threat of war between North and South Korea.[16] "Pull" factors such as improved economic and educational opportunities as part of the "American Dream"—along with increased economic, military, and political ties between South Korea and the United States—contributed to the steady flow of South Korean immigrants. Unlike Koreans in China, Koreans in the United States are not concentrated in one geographic area. Sociologists Pyong Gap Min and Chigon Kim estimate that roughly half a million Korean Americans reside in California, which is nearly 30 percent of the total Korean population in the United States, and almost half of all Korean Americans live in seven major metropolitan areas: Los Angeles; New York City; Washington, DC; San Francisco; Chicago; Philadelphia; and Honolulu.[17] This concentration is mirrored within the Korean American sample in this study, as nearly three-fourths of the respondents are from the Los Angeles–Orange County region, the New York City–New Jersey–Connecticut region, or the northern Virginia area near Washington, DC.

Creating Koreanness in China and the United States

The differing emigration histories of Korean Americans and Korean Chinese have a significant impact on their orientations to the Korean peninsula. As second- and third-generation immigrants, Korean Chinese in the study are aware their parents or grandparents left before the establishment of North and South Korea. They generally frame their ancestors' decision to immigrate to

China as a "forced" rather than voluntary decision. Their "exiled" status in China after WWII and the Korean War and their historical involvement in the Korean independence movement in Manchuria was evidence of their strong orientation to the Korean peninsula and a unified "Korean" nation. Most Korean Chinese in this study have had sustained contact with relatives in North Korea rather than South Korea. In fact, Chul Mu, a Korean Chinese man, believes most Korean Chinese have a "bigger sense of affinity with North Korea." Korean Chinese use "*hanguk*" to refer to South Korea, "*bukhan*" or "*eebuk*" for North Korea, and "Joseon" for their homeland, which encompasses the entirety of the Korean peninsula.

In contrast, Korean emigrants to the United States after the Korean War left an already divided peninsula. Korean Americans use "Korean" and "Korea" almost exclusively to refer to South Korea, linguistically aligning their identities with their parents' former South Korean citizenship. This is perhaps unsurprising given that few Korean Americans retained ties to North Korean relatives and were largely raised in households that were staunchly anticommunist and highly critical of the North Korean regime. Furthermore, in 2002, President Bush's inclusion of North Korea in the "axis of evil" (along with Iran and Iraq) in his State of the Union Address made any sympathies with North Korea akin to an unequivocal support for antidemocratic, rogue nations. Ideas about Koreanness among 1.5- and second-generation Korean American respondents are largely created from the memories of their parents of an underdeveloped South Korea in the 1960s and 1970s. They stress the voluntary nature of their family's decision to emigrate, citing the "American Dream" and the greater economic and educational opportunities in the United States as compared to South Korea.

Levels of language fluency are more varied for Korean Americans than Korean Chinese. Korean Americans often use the term "Konglish," a mixture of English and Korean, in reference to the primary language in their homes. Commonly in the case of Korean Americans with very low verbal abilities, their parents speak to them in Korean while they respond in English. Even with relatively low levels of Korean reading, writing, and speaking proficiency, most Korean Americans nevertheless retain medium to high levels of oral comprehension. In contrast, the particular context of Yanbian, with its unique national minority educational systems and geographic concentration of ethnic Koreans, means that most Korean Chinese up through the third generation are equally fluent in both Korean and Chinese. They speak of linguistic switching depending on the context—using Korean in school and within the home and Chinese in other public areas.

Despite these clear differences, most Korean Americans and Korean Chinese in the study express strong emotional and cultural ties to a Koreanness that is complicated by geopolitics but not bound to it. Much of this is attributed to the retention of deeply ingrained cultural practices they identified as distinctly "Korean" within the family and household, such as language and food, the regular celebration of Korean holidays, and visits by relatives as well as trips to the Korean peninsula. For example, many grew up speaking or at least hearing Korean in the home and eating "three square Korean meals a day," featuring traditional Korean dishes like *kimchee*, a spicy fermented cabbage side dish, and *doenjang jjigae*, a Korean miso-based stew.

As a third-generation Korean Chinese woman, Chung Ae believes that "it is important to preserve these Korean customs and traditions because . . . we [South Koreans and Korean Chinese] are the same people. Until reunification happens, traditional ties are necessary to bind people together." Many Korean Americans and Korean Chinese perform adapted annual ceremonies over important Korean holidays like *chuseok* and *seolnal*.[18] Chul Mu, a third-generation Korean Chinese man, says for chuseok, his family "would set up memorial tables for our ancestors . . . go and tidy the graves up a bit, pour alcohol, bow." Catherine, a second-generation Korean American woman, says her entire extended family in the New York area celebrates seolnal together every year, which means that they eat traditional soup with flattened oval rice cakes called *ddukguk* and children bow to their elders in a practice known as *saebae* in exchange for money. As a child, Catherine remembers hording these precious envelopes from her aunts, uncles, and grandparents, opening them from time to time to count and recount her money. More than a set of rituals that take place in individual households, these practices and behaviors serve as an important connection between Koreans everywhere, both in the diaspora and in the homeland.

Controlling Koreanness
INSTITUTIONAL POLICIES IN CHINA

With a diverse population of over a billion people, the Chinese state explicitly ties the central promise of citizenship to the guaranteed protection of recognized national minority groups. The constitution of the People's Republic of China states that "each nationality possesses equal rights in such areas as politics, economy, culture, language, religion, and more. Any one nationality is prohibited from enjoying special prerogatives."[19] Beginning with five formally recognized minority groups—Han, Tibetans, Manchus, Mongols, and Hui—today the list has expanded to fifty-five *minzu*, or different national groups.[20] By 1989, the Chinese government established 141 autonomous geographic regions, 5 at the provincial level, 31 autonomous prefectures (such as Yanbian), and 105 autonomous counties or banners.[21] In addition, the Autonomy Law passed in 1984 granted privileges to national minorities, such as the right to maintain nationality schools as well as their own language, customs, and traditions. Other benefits included affirmative action policies in hiring and promotion practices in the workplace, lower minimum scores on college entrance exams, and educational subsidies. National minorities are also exempted from national family planning policies such as the "one-child" rule.

It is important to note that China's position on cultural pluralism has not always been so generous. Beginning with the Great Leap Forward and continuing through the Cultural Revolution, policies of forced assimilation meant no special treatment was granted for minorities and the preservation of minority linguistic and cultural traditions was strongly discouraged. During this period, state-sponsored educational systems were used to indoctrinate younger generations with a specific political ideology, Chinese history, and geography, and "nationality schools" in areas with high concentrations of minority groups were dissolved.[22] Historian Frank Dikotter noted that "within popular culture, scientific circles and government publications" from the late 1970s and 1980s, ethnic Han were represented as "a more highly evolved and better endowed nation-race" while national minorities were "less evolved branches of people who need the moral and political guidance of the 'Han' in order to ascend on the scales of civilization."[23]

While national policies promoting cultural pluralism were reinstated following the Cultural Revolution, research has documented significant political, social, and economic inequalities between ethnic Han and national minority populations within China when controlling for linguistic, ethnic, religious, and geographic differences.[24] Regions with the highest concentration of minorities are often the poorest with lowered living standards. Generally, national minorities have shorter life expectancies and fewer economic and educational opportunities than their ethnic Han counterparts. Ethnic Koreans in China are a notable exception. They are generally viewed as "model minorities" compared to other national minority groups in China.[25] Korean Chinese have high levels of Korean literacy and what is considered one of the best educational systems among minority groups in China. Korean Chinese have nearly 100 percent attendance at the primary school level in contrast to other minorities, such as Tibetans, who have only 50.4 percent attendance.[26] In 1949, Yanbian University was established in Yanji as one of the first institutions of higher learning for national minorities. As a result, Korean Chinese have maintained a strong sense of ethnic identity, particularly in terms of language and cultural preservation.[27]

Political scientist Enze Han notes three key ways Korean Chinese differ from other Chinese minority groups in his comparative analysis of five Chinese national minority groups—Uyghurs, Korean Chinese, Mongols, the Dai, and Tibetans. First, Korean

Chinese have relatively recent immigration histories to China and are not indigenous to the land in which they currently reside.[28] Second, they have strong external cultural ties to two "kin states," North and South Korea. However, while many Korean Chinese have since migrated to South Korea for economic opportunities in pursuit of the "Korean Dream," they receive very little explicit political support from either North or South Korea, both of which are largely uninvolved with Korean Chinese affairs in China. Third, Korean Chinese labor migrants who return to China circulate stories about their direct experiences with marginalization and poor treatment at the hands of South Koreans. As a result, Han concludes that Korean Chinese are more likely to adapt to their status in China rather than engage in "national contestation" like Tibetans and Uyghurs, whose resistance movements have been subject to well-publicized militarized response by the Chinese state. Using survey data conducted in Hunchun, a city in Yanbian Prefecture, Han finds that most Korean Chinese respondents report little conflict between their ethnic identity as Koreans and their citizenship as Chinese, choosing to "treat both Koreas as their motherland (*guguo*), and China as their fatherland (*zuguo*)."[29]

My conversations with Korean Chinese about their identities generally fall in line with Han's findings. Many respondents echo the official state doctrine nearly verbatim as evidence for the lack of conflict between their Korean and Chinese identities. For example, Hee Sook, a Korean Chinese woman in her early thirties, says, "In China, there are many different races. The nation protects and maintains these cultural differences. . . . It is understood that Korean Chinese have Chinese citizenship but roots in the Korean peninsula."[30] She grew up in the city of Yeongil[31] in Yanbian and lived in a mixed neighborhood of ethnic Han and Korean Chinese where "everything is intermingled. . . . [Even] the signposts are in Chinese and Korean." In fact, Hee Sook jokes that Yeongil could be mistaken for any city in South Korea given the visible presence of Korean culture in public spaces. Overall, few of those interviewed state that their Koreanness is a significant hindrance to their social, economic, and political mobility and are generally cautious about comments that could be construed as critical of the Chinese state.

But a deeper analysis of the interviews offers hints of underlying tensions experienced by Korean Chinese in a country that is over 90 percent ethnic Han. While the number of Korean Chinese in China is estimated at roughly two million, this translates to roughly 2 percent of the total ethnic minority population and barely 0.1 percent of the total population.[32] It is perhaps unsurprising that many seem to equate "real" Chineseness with being ethnically Han, similar to the ways Korean Americans see whiteness as a defining quality of "real" Americanness. There are a few examples of direct tension between Korean Chinese and ethnic Han, who remain the numerical majority even in the three northeast provinces where ethnic Koreans are concentrated. For example, Myeong Dae grew up in a town in Yanbian. With a laugh, he says he fought often with ethnic Han classmates as a child because they "would make fun of me because I wasn't Han." Similarly, Chul Mu notes that "[in] my hometown in China, there's a Korean Chinese neighborhood and a Han Chinese neighborhood, and they are always fighting against each other." He says there was an understanding that "you shouldn't mess with Korean Chinese. If you touch one, grandpas and kids will run out to defend whoever is being messed with. That's why they're scary." However, because ethnic Han outnumber Korean Chinese, Chul Mu ruefully admits that the results generally favored the former—but that the latter always put up a good fight.

While these fights between youths did not seem to escalate into more serious tensions, the line dividing Han Chinese and Korean Chinese continues to manifest in their social lives. Most Korean Chinese, particularly those living in Yanbian, have predominantly Korean Chinese social networks suggesting an informal segregation among peers. Additionally, most second- and third-generation respondents say they are strongly encouraged by their parents to date and marry a fellow Korean Chinese over an ethnic Han. This implies that ethnic difference continues to remain salient despite the absence of explicit stories like those shared by

Korean Americans about their encounters with institutional and individual acts of racism and discrimination.

But there are other signs that Korean Chinese communities are succumbing to assimilation pressures in China. The overall population of Korean Chinese in Yanbian has declined steadily due to outmigration both abroad as well as to major Chinese urban cities. This has had a noticeable impact on Korean Chinese communities. For example, between 1990 and 2002, the number of primary schools dropped from 386 to 162, and the number of middle schools had also declined from 112 to 82 despite their strong reputations.[33] Korean Chinese I speak with have seen attendance at these schools drop beyond the third generation for practical reasons. As Chung Ae explains, "In the past, most parents chose to send their children to Korean Chinese schools. But in the end, if you want to attend college or work in a Chinese firm, then you need to be able to speak Chinese fluently. So these days . . . going to a Korean Chinese school is a slight disadvantage." A second-generation man notes the generational and cultural divide within his family as a result of his children's lack of interest in learning Korean, "Nowadays, when children play, they just use Chinese. They don't use Korean at all; it's not necessary . . . It's like the US—you don't need to learn Korean." The loss of cultural and linguistic knowledge has eroded the social distance between ethnic Han and Korean Chinese, signaling a potential shift away from Koreanness as a salient identity in future generations.

While they benefit from official protections for national minorities, the lives of Korean Chinese are heavily constrained by the household, or *hukou*, registration system. All Chinese citizens are classified as an agricultural, or "peasant," household (*nongye hukou*) or an urban household (*chengshijumin hukou*), a division strictly enforced by the state.[34] Instituted as part of the first Five-Year Plan in 1955, the goal of the hukou program continues to be the prevention of widespread migration of rural residents to urban areas, which would overload available housing, educational, medical, and social services. The application process is complicated for rural residents who wish to migrate domestically while still retaining the full benefits of citizenship. Internal migrants must secure temporary resident permits from the urban police and local government, and their employers must also apply for legal work permits and secure legal documents for their employees.[35] Despite strict regulations, a growing "floating population" of an estimated sixty to eighty million undocumented Chinese have migrated to cities searching for work.[36]

The hukou system may be negating some of the benefits Korean Chinese gain from policies designed to protect national minorities. On one hand, living in Yanbian Korean Autonomous Prefecture—a region officially granted to ethnic Koreans in China—means that Koreanness is protected through strong institutionalized support systems. On the other hand, Yanbian has fewer economic and educational opportunities than coastal areas like Shenzhen, which have been transformed into major hubs of economic development by an influx of resources and foreign investment in the last few decades. Yanbian also lacks the prestige of urban megacities like Shanghai and Beijing, which are at the heart of the political, economic, and social activities within the country.

For Korean Chinese and other national minorities residing in predominantly rural or urban areas far from the industrial and manufacturing centers in China, the hukou system institutionalizes unequal opportunities indirectly as a result of their ethnic identities despite their Chinese citizenship. In Hee Sook's case, her decision to move abroad was highly influenced by the fact that hukou status is determined by matrilineal descent and is very difficult to change. Following graduation from a university in Beijing, Hee Sook was required to return to her hometown in Yanbian Prefecture because "In China, it's where you are born and where your mother lives that counts. . . . My mom is from Yeongil [in Yanbian], therefore I am from Yeongil." Hee Sook continues, "Resources are allocated by areas, and you can't change your registered hometown. In the past, I heard that if you had money, you [could] change it. Now that's not possible." Upon their return to their hometowns, many college graduates like Hee Sook find few economic opportunities to apply their skills and knowledge. Although some of her college classmates went on to graduate programs in Japan, the United States, and Canada, Hee Sook chose to pursue her master's degree in South Korea, given her Korean cultural and linguistic fluency and its geographic proximity to Yanbian and her family.

Overall, the lack of upward mobility in Yanbian and Northeast China more broadly translates into a de facto partial citizenship for Korean Chinese. Coupled with the constraints on domestic mobility due to the household (hukou) registration system, international migration becomes an attractive option for residents of underdeveloped, resource-poor regions like Yanbian. For Korean Chinese, South Korea is a popular destination. Increased educational and economic opportunities and higher standards of living as well as high levels of Korean cultural capital have brought a steady flow of Korean Chinese to South Korea since the 1980s in what has been called the "Korean wind." While the enactment of diversity policies in China differs significantly from the US context, the result for Korean Chinese I meet is notably similar to that of Korean Americans—migration to South Korea.

INSTITUTIONAL POLICIES IN THE UNITED STATES

"I remember my mom saying I had to study twice as hard and my English had to be better than other people's English, because I was Korean, not White. That I had to do everything twice as good because of racism and stuff. . . . Being Korean was viewed as a negative in certain respects because of societal disadvantages." This is how Daniel, a second-generation Korean American man, explains the burdens of being racialized and ethnically marked as a person of color and child of immigrants in the United States. How is it that Daniel can feel so alienated and be forced to work twice as hard to be accepted in a nation that prides itself on its immigrant roots and makes diversity at the center of what it means to be American?

In practice, what it means to be as "American as apple pie" is defined by a dominant, nonethnic culture centered on whiteness. Scholars have argued that local, state, and federal legislation have largely minimized the threat of difference by promoting a sense of cultural "sameness" within its citizenry. Immigration policies are a key example of this. In 2017, the proposed immigration policies of US president Donald Trump include promises to build a wall along the US–Mexico border, to institute a "Muslim ban" by restricting the entry of people from "the most dangerous and volatile regions of the world that have a history of exporting terrorism," and to admit only "those who share our values and respect our people."[37] The message is intrinsically racialized: those of specific religious faiths or nations of origin present a clear and present danger to national security, and "our" values and "our" people is read as those of Whites.

Historically, there have been numerous restrictions against immigrants from non-European countries of origin. For example, immigrants from Asia have been subjected to successive and increasingly exclusionary policies beginning with the Page Law in 1875 and the Chinese Exclusion Act of 1882. The passage of the 1907 Gentleman's Agreement restricted Japanese immigration to the United States and included Koreans as Japanese colonial subjects. Under the Immigration Act of 1917, known as the Asiatic Barred Zone Act, restrictions expanded to include most of Central Asia, South Asia, and Southeast Asia. This was followed by the Immigration Act of 1924, which prevented the entry of Asian immigrants on the basis that they were "aliens ineligible for citizenship."[38] Unlike European immigrants during this same period, the growing "hordes" of unfamiliar Asian immigrants provoked nativist fears of an economic, political, and cultural takeover—the "Yellow Peril." These policies had the dual effects of continuously marking Asians as "perpetual foreigners" and potential threats to America and American culture throughout the twenty-first century.[39]

The Immigration Act of 1965 permanently changed the landscape of US race and ethnic relations, opening borders to "new" immigrants largely from Asia, Latin America, and the Caribbean. The "melting pot" metaphor of assimilation gave way to the "salad bowl" of cultural pluralism. Diversity was touted as the source of national strength, yet within carefully controlled limits.

As sociologist Monisha Das Gupta argues, the ideology of multiculturalism "glides over the actual relationships between and within cultures in contact in the United States."[40] Within "safe" avenues of "fun, food and festivals" and within designated spaces, more Americans began celebrating diverse holidays such as Lunar New Year or Diwali (the Hindu Festival of Lights) and attending programming by months including "Black History Month" in February and "Asian Pacific American Heritage Month" in May. Multiculturalism in this context reinforces the notion that "difference" is constituted against a White, Eurocentric norm. There are no designated heritage months for Europeans, and the most prominent US holidays, like the Fourth of July and Thanksgiving, celebrate the achievements of early European American settlers.

In addition to national policies that carefully calibrate spaces of cultural pluralism, legislation continues to push a shared "American" national culture centered on whiteness, particularly in states along the US–Mexico border with high immigrant populations. Historian Vijay Prashad points to proposed English-only policies in the workplace, in schools, and even for driver's license tests and voting ballots as examples of "pragmatic racism" designed to disempower immigrants.[41] Other examples include the erosion of bilingual education initiatives such as Proposition 227, named "English for the Children," in 1998. California voters passed this initiative to ban bilingual education, in effect making English the de facto official language. Ironically, the study of *foreign* languages is allowed and encouraged in the standard US educational curriculum. A more recent example was HB 2281 in Arizona in 2013. This bill upheld a ban on the offering of ethnic studies courses, particularly a Mexican American studies curriculum, in Tucson schools because it was said to "promote resentment toward a race," presumably Whites. Supporters of this bill argued these classes were "designed for students of a particular ethnicity," which neatly sidestepped any acknowledgement that the traditional curriculum reflected the interests of the dominant racial group.[42] Institutionalized xenophobia and nativism inherent in these educational policies promote an ethnically neutral, Eurocentric notion of Americanness that smooths over differences and forces immigrants to assimilate into the dominant culture.[43]

Institutional policies that make whiteness normative contribute to the general perceptions by the public about who constitutes an "outsider" in the United States, which can take on ascribed racial characteristics. For Korean Americans in the study, this comes through in informal interactions with White Americans. For example, Paula, a Korean American woman in her early twenties, recalls dealing with the commonly asked "Where are you really from?" question as early as elementary school: "People would ask where I was from and I would always say 'I'm from here,' like America. 'No, where are you really from?' 'Planet Earth,' because I was just really offended." Similar examples come up frequently in separate conversations with other Korean Americans. For many, the emphasis on "really" implies that they aren't from "here" simply because of their physical appearance. By repeatedly answering with their hometowns in the United States or deliberately misunderstanding the question as Paula does, many Korean Americans indirectly challenge people on the double-edged nature of the query or force them to restate the motivations behind their inquiry. While some acknowledged that the question may have reflected genuine curiosity, most Korean Americans interpret it as a way of highlighting their minority racial status and their presumed recent immigrant histories. It is particularly telling because they notice that none of their White peers are subject to the same line of questioning. Racial logics and the assumption of whiteness as the de facto standard for Americanness mean Asians will always be alien and foreign.

The related practice of hyphenation in categories like "Asian-American," "African-American," and "Native-American" also highlights the normative power of whiteness given the near-absence of the comparable term "European-American." Sociologists Stanley Lieberson and Mary Waters use the term, "unhyphenated whites," to refer to people who "are able or willing to identify themselves solely as whites, and who have little or no interest in or knowledge of their European ancestry or origin."[44] Maya, who was born and raised in the US, is well aware that identifying as "just American" without hyphenation is not a choice for her. She expresses her frustration in this way: "African American, Chinese American, Korean American. Why do we have to be that and White people are just American? Why can't they be Irish, Scottish, German American?" She continues by calling out the privileges of whiteness: "And they think it's strange if I ask them about their roots. [They say], 'Of course, I'm just American.'" Their minoritized status as people of color is perceived as an impediment to upward mobility and accompanied by feelings of permanent marginalization in the United States.[45] Similarly, Herb says, "America never felt like home . . . because I'm not White. If I really want to be president, I can't. But that was one of my aspirations, until I realized that I am Korean. I mean, I'm a US citizen . . . but mostly likely I won't have those opportunities because of my color."

For many Korean Americans with whom I speak, their first direct experiences with the stigmas attached to being from an immigrant family occurred within the American school system. Paula recounts the shame of being assigned to English as a Second Language (ESL) classes in early elementary school, "Because everything is in Korean [at home], I [couldn't] comprehend English sometimes. Up until first grade, I was in ESL." Paula says her parents "freaked out" and instituted "an 'English only' rule for the house." Korean Americans quickly learn at school that speaking English without an accent is essential to be accepted as American. Herb often found himself in the role of a translator between his mother and his teacher. He remembered, "The other kids asked if my mom was retarded. . . . [They] said my mom was stupid; 'she can't even speak English.'" His face reddens at the memory, "It was so embarrassing, 'my mom can't talk with other people,' you feel inferior too. These White people are better than me. I look different already, now I know that we're valued less." Herb internalized the assumption that visible markers of being part of an immigrant family means being subordinate to a dominant standard defined by whiteness.

Korean Americans, particularly men, share racialized experiences in the contexts of profiling by law enforcement and verbal or physical confrontations with Whites. Sae Il, a biracial second-generation Korean American in his thirties, offers a literal example of racist labeling. He grew up in a small, working-class town in Ohio as one of a few non-White residents. His brother played in a youth football league, and Sae Il noted that "the coach . . . wrote everybody's last names on their helmet, except my brother's. On his helmet, he wrote 'Chink,' and that is what my brother was called from that point onwards." Although his brother was not offended by this practice and even embraced the nickname throughout high school, Sae Il saw it very differently. For him, it was an example of his town's permissive attitudes toward blatant racism, made worse by the fact that "Chink" was a pejorative term for Chinese rather than Koreans. Herb provides two examples of racism and racial profiling as an Asian American in predominantly White settings. He says, "Growing up in a rich White neighborhood, . . . we used to have race fights in our school. We [Asians] were outnumbered." Another time, he was pulled over in his White, upper-middle-class neighborhood by a police officer, who "punked" him, saying, "I pulled you over because your taillight is out." The officer grabbed the pack of cigarettes on the dashboard before letting Herb go. Later that evening, Herb saw that his lights were fine but that the officer "pulled me over just to mess with me. . . . because of how I looked. . . . That's when I feel [South] Korea is my home."

Clashes between Koreans and other communities of color, in particular, the so-called Black–Korean conflict, further accentuate the precarious social location of Korean immigrants and Korean Americans who are, in the words of sociologist Pyong Gap Min, "caught in the middle" between whiteness and blackness.[46] Research on Black–Korean hostilities have focused on two events that received national attention. The first was the 1990 boycott of Korean-owned grocers in Flatbush, Brooklyn, by Black community members in response to repeated acts of discrimination and violence committed against customers. The second was the Los Angeles Rebellion in 1992 after the Rodney King verdict was released.[47] In both cases, Korean immigrants were criticized for profiting from predominantly Black and/or low-income neighborhoods without reinvesting back into the community both economically and socially. These high-profile incidents fueled the perception that Korean immigrants were achieving upward mobility through the oppression of Blacks within the US racial order. The dominant analysis of these conflicts and one adopted by many Koreans themselves is that they were "victims" or "scapegoats" of violence perpetrated by "out of control" Black and Brown looters engaging in wanton destruction of property. Many scholars have critiqued this simplistic framework for ignoring the ways systematic racism and discrimination ultimately pitted Koreans and Blacks in low-income neighborhoods against each other as they competed for scarce resources.[48] Like myself, many Korean American respondents who grew up in Los Angeles in the 1990s vividly remembered the smoke from the fires that dotted the city landscape, especially in the area around Koreatown. Conflicts like these weakened their faith in the promises of the American Dream that drew their parents to the United States in the 1970s.

While Korean Americans struggle with their vulnerable position within US racial logics, they also grapple with internal policing from within their own community. The "FOB" versus "twinkie" dichotomy speaks to the challenges of striking the right balance being "too assimilated" and "unassimilable." "FOB" is a slang term that stands for "fresh off the boat," referring to recent immigrants who, as one Korean American puts it, "don't look like they are ever going to adapt to America." Having a social network composed of primarily other Asians during one's adolescence and college years puts one at risk of being labeled a "FOB." Other nondesirable behaviors associated with being too "fobby" are listening almost exclusively to Korean popular music (K-pop), watching Korean dramas, or speaking English with an accent.[49] These visible markers of foreignness demonstrate an inability to assimilate to dominant American culture.

At the other end of the spectrum, those who are "too Americanized" or "White-washed" are also held in contempt by Korean American respondents who believe in the importance of maintaining a connection to being Korean without assimilating completely. Common slang terms like "banana" and "twinkie" are used by respondents to mean "yellow on the outside, White on the inside"—in other words, "too White."[50] As a result, Korean Americans simultaneously uphold whiteness as the standard for Americanness while also challenging the assumption that total assimilation is a desired goal. Catherine's experience of being called a "twinkie" highlights the tensions over how much Koreanness is considered too much, how much is not enough, and who gets to decide. As someone who generally did not have Asian American friends in high school, Catherine felt constantly judged by the Korean Americans who "kind of looked down on me. . . . call[ed] me 'twinkie' and that whole thing." The "FOB"–"twinkie" debate speaks to a no-win situation for Korean Americans where the middle ground is difficult to define and impossible to achieve.

Despite educational and immigration policies that ostensibly promote multiculturalism and diversity, second-generation Korean Americans experience a reality that devalues immigrant and ethnic identities. Questions about their "real" origins, their hyphenated statuses, the trauma of being placed in ESL or being teased for their parents' lack of fluency in English are constant reminders of their vulnerable position in a country that simultaneously embraces and rejects them. Continued conflict with Whites and Blacks as well within the Korean American community itself means defending their Americanness from external and internal attacks. Many Korean Americans imagine their return to South Korea as an escape to an uncomplicated space in which they will be freed from the burdens of minority status and its attendant challenges. Discouraged by repeated experiences with direct and indirect forms of racism and discrimination, they begin to consider return migration seriously.

Conclusion

In summary, there are two main aspects of the premigration condition that fuel return migration projects for both Korean Americans and Korean Chinese. First is the presence of existing networks to South Korea. For Korean Americans who have relatives living in South Korea, friends who moved there previously, or who have visited previously, South Korea is a familiar, less daunting destination for migration. While most Korean Chinese have not had substantive connections with South Korean relatives, many do have ties to family members, friends, former coworkers, or college classmates who have gone to Seoul for jobs or graduate programs. Additionally, the spread of South Korean popular culture, especially dramas, as well as news programs in China have kept Korean Chinese up to date with current political, economic, and social conditions. Very few Korean American or Korean Chinese respondents decide to "return" to South Korea without one or more of these existing ties.

Second is a strong emotional identification with South Korea as an ancestral homeland. Many Korean Chinese and Korean Americans in the study use *primordial* arguments to frame Koreanness as something innate, undiluted by their immigration histories, and powerful enough to transcend the bonds of citizenship. Regardless of cultural and linguistic knowledge, Koreanness becomes an absolute identity, unchanged by American or Chinese citizenship. As Paula puts it, "My mom would always tell [my siblings and me] that your blood is Korean, but you are American." Despite numerous experiences with racism and discrimination, this logic allows Korean Americans and Korean Chinese to conceive of their ethnic and national identities as complementary, rather than contradictory.

For both sets of return migrants, blood as a key characteristic of Koreanness, coupled with their emigration histories, provides incontrovertible proof of their ties to the Korean peninsula regardless of their nationality. Some imagine South Korea as a national context in which the racial and ethnic manifestation of their Koreanness will make them a part of the dominant rather than the minority group. In the absence of substantive experiences with the homeland, as well as the inevitable loss of some Korean cultural capital over time, they still can claim ethnic membership as a Korean regardless of citizenship and cultural knowledge. Their Korean identities and existing networks allow them to access a broader set of global options in the face of limitations in the United States and China.

In this chapter, I have outlined the ways Koreanness is created, controlled, negotiated, and reclaimed within the contexts of the United States and China. The premigration condition sheds light on the ways the "homeland" is constructed by second- and later-generation immigrants based on the specific time and context of their families' emigration histories. Also important is how "Koreanness" is experienced in the "home" countries of the United States and China at the institutional level as a result of state policies regarding diversity and cultural pluralism as well as at the personal level within the family, among friends, and in immigrant communities. The idea of South Korea as a homeland, a strong Korean identity, and the realities of limited economic mobility, a tight job market, and existing pathways to South Korea forged by previous migrants all act as important factors that fuel "returns." Many Korean Americans and Korean Chinese turn their sights abroad to the global market at a moment when South Korea offers a high standard of living, higher wages, and greater job opportunities. However, as will become clear in the next four chapters, their "homecomings" to South Korea prove to be bittersweet.

2

Return Migrants in the South Korean Immigration System and Labor Market

After one of my English classes at the Korean Chinese church, I join a group of men around a table in the lounge area with a helpful introduction by Chul Mu, a staff member who is well known and respected in this community. He explains that I am a Korean American doing research on Korean Chinese in South Korea. After brief nods of acknowledgement, the men continue their conversation, though a sense of unease is palpable given the unexpected presence of an interloper who is not only a woman but also not Korean Chinese. Every so often, I can sense a few furtive glances in my direction, but after about ten minutes, the group seems to relax and ignore my presence. I am concentrating hard, feeling one step behind as I take in their non-Seoul accents and translate in my head. At some point, one of the men launches into an extended rant about the difficulties renewing his visa, including missing a day of work to spend hours waiting in line with no guarantee of approval. Turning in my direction, he says, "You're a US citizen, right? What kind of visa are you on?" And suddenly all eyes are on me. After an awkward silence, he asks me to pull out my official South Korean immigration card. He slips his own out of his wallet and puts our cards side by side on the table in the middle of the group. He points to the top line on my card, which has the Korean characters for "foreign" (*oeguk*), "nationality" (*gukjeok*), and what loosely translates to "overseas brethren" (*dongpo*).[1] With his finger still above this last word, he asks in a raised voice tinged with frustration and some anger, "Why should your card have 'dongpo' on it while mine doesn't? How come Korean Americans like you get that label while I can't?" It is a good question. While I recognize his antagonism is not directed at me personally, all I can do is stare down at the cards, my cheeks burning with embarrassment as the other men voice their agreement. The conversation continues to other matters, but still feeling uncomfortable from the exchange, I gather my belongings and quietly excuse myself.

The resentment of those Korean Chinese men speaks to larger tensions around the narrow criteria used by the South Korean state to determine who is or is not legally recognized as dongpo. If the ancestral ties of Korean Chinese, like those of Korean Americans, can be traced to the Korean peninsula, why are the former systematically excluded while the latter are not? At issue are the contentious hierarchies institutionalized within the South Korean immigration system. Migrant workers are subject to a sorting process in the South Korean labor market and visa system along two axes: one that separates skilled from unskilled workers and a second that defines foreigners from family using an explicitly *South Korean* definition of family. These two distinctions are *formally* defined at the institutional level through South Korean immigration policies, which then determine where these migrants get slotted within the South Korean labor market. This, in turn, shapes general perceptions of Korean Chinese and Korean Americans and impacts their *informal* interactions with South Korean employers and coworkers.

In this chapter, I explore how categories like "skilled" worker versus "unskilled" worker and "foreigner" versus "family" as designated by dongpo, as well as *gyopo* and *minjok*, significantly shape the economic and social positions of Korean Chinese and Korean Americans in Seoul. I show that Korean Americans accrue greater economic, social, and legal privileges as skilled professional workers and are widely viewed by South Koreans as dongpo—part of the Korean "family." In contrast, Korean Chinese are concentrated mainly in low-wage, low-status manual labor jobs. Furthermore, their classification as "foreigners," rather than "dongpo," has negative social and economic consequences for them as workers.

Hierarchical Nationhood at Work

Sociologists Dong-Hoon Seol and John Skrentny use "hierarchical nationhood" to reference the "more and less inclusive" practices by nation-states in relation to coethnic return migrants that rely on a combination of "co-nationality with economic utility."[2] They argue that South Korea's immigration policies, like those of Germany and Greece, maximize economic benefits to the "host" nation by making distinctions between coethnic immigrants based on their nation of origin. Visa categories favor workers from "top-tier," highly developed capitalist countries like Japan and the United States with valuable, specialized skills over those with more general skill sets from lower-tier communist countries with uneven economic development like China and Russia.[3]

These hierarchies have social dimensions as well. Hierarchical nationhood operates on "a simultaneous recognition, on either the part of the state or the public or both, of sameness and difference on a key trait."[4] Seol and Skrentny's findings include the results of a survey of South Korean citizens that shows that they are significantly more likely to view Korean Americans as dongpo or "family" as compared to Korean Chinese. For return migrants, coethnicity matters less to the Korean nation-state than their perceived economic contribution. Overall, the Korean Americans I spoke with are uniformly concentrated into professional, skilled positions that most South Koreans cannot perform. With few exceptions, the Korean Chinese I met at the church are in physically demanding jobs in unskilled/semiskilled labor that middle class, upwardly mobile South Koreans do not want to do. The deep disparities between Korean Americans and Korean Chinese in Seoul highlight the ways *nationality*, rather than coethnicity, becomes a crucial factor in shaping their work lives.

South Korea is one of four countries that quickly industrialized in the latter half of the twentieth century, collectively known as the "Asian Tigers." Following what was called the "Miracle on the Han River," South Korea experienced steady increases in economic growth and prosperity. Yet the 1997 Asian financial crisis forced South Korea to institute neoliberal reforms in exchange for loans from the International Monetary Fund that resulted in a dramatic restructuring of the South Korean labor market and the opening of borders to foreign migrant workers.[5] Ranked in the top twenty economies worldwide by gross domestic product (GDP) and fourth in Asia after China, Japan, and India, South Korea has transformed into a destination point for labor migrants drawn by employment opportunities in both skilled and unskilled industries such as manufacturing, construction, business, finance, and teaching.[6] The reliance on foreign workers led to the creation of new visa policies that regulated their entry and controlled their political and social participation in larger South Korean society.

According to a 2012 government survey, the number of foreigners above the age of fifteen living in South Korea is currently over 1.2 million, reflecting a steady increase over the past few decades.[7] Among foreign workers, Korean Chinese comprise the highest percentage by nationality, followed by Vietnamese and Chinese (non–Korean Chinese), with workers from the United States and Canada rounding out the top four. The total number of employed foreigners entering on the "Overseas Korean" F-4 visa is 99,000.[8] As noted in the opening story of this chapter, Korean Chinese do not generally qualify for this category. While these data presumably reflect only documented foreign workers, the statistics suggest that the flow of foreigners coming to work in South Korea, especially Korean Chinese, has remained steady, particularly in unskilled and semiskilled industries.

The favorable combination of coethnicity, educational credentials, and US linguistic capital allows Korean Americans to find employment easily in Seoul, particularly as teachers. Like many Korean Americans I spoke with, Gloria works as an SAT[9] tutor in Seoul at a *hagwon*, or "cram school." Common in South Korea, these private learning academies offer instruction in a wide range of academic subjects, including English language, math, and preparation for standardized exams, as well as nonacademic subjects like cooking, painting, and flower arranging. Although Gloria's college degree and previous work experiences are a plus, she says being a native English speaker is her most valuable asset as a worker. As she explains, "They [South Koreans] prize the idea of being able to speak English. . . . You get money to talk; that's why so many Korean Americans come here."

The "English craze" has led to a dramatic increase in employment opportunities in hagwon, high schools, and universities in South Korea. In addition, privileged elementary, middle school, and high school students with aspirations of attending US universities and colleges look to private tutoring and hagwon to increase their scores on college entrance exams like the TOEFL[10], ACT[11], and SAT. Graduates from elite American schools are seen as the perfect resource to craft better-quality application materials like personal statements in an increasingly competitive admissions process, especially for international students. Like Gloria, many Korean Americans take advantage of these job openings by using their linguistic capital as well as the status granted by undergraduate and graduate degrees from prominent US colleges and universities. Paula, a teacher at an exclusive English-only high school, says, "Koreans like social status. They like teachers from good schools. If you came from Harvard, you can walk on campus and they would hire you." Herb, a teacher at an English hagwon in the ritzy area of Apgujeong, believes "the reputation of [University of California,] Berkeley"—where he received his undergraduate degree—"is more important than being gyopo"[12] (a descendant of former *South* Korean citizens living abroad). Korean American language teachers are often assumed to be qualified for these jobs even without formal training or relevant teaching experience.

Foreign language instructors enter on visa categories such as the E-1 for professors at the university level and E-2 for teachers at hagwon and elementary, middle, and high schools. In addition to the employment contract signed by the sponsoring school or educational facility, these visa holders need to provide official documentation of educational credentials, such as a college diploma, as well as a "letter of personal security assurance," which proves they are financially able to provide for themselves. Outside of the teaching and college preparatory industries, South Korean companies looking to build a strong global presence in the areas of business, finance, and banking hire foreign professionals on C-2 or C-4 visas. Again, Americans are valued for the cultural capital that South Koreans perceive as valuable in today's global economy, such as relevant work experience, native English speaking skills, and informal knowledge of Western business practices. The experiences of Korean Americans, who are almost exclusively engaged in white-collar work of this kind, differ considerably from that of Korean Chinese labor migrants.

Korean Chinese Manual Workers

According to the 2013 Foreigner Labour Force survey, there are an estimated 760,000 employed foreigners in South Korea, of which roughly 377,000 work in manufacturing. An additional 138,000 are employed in "Business, Personal and Public Services," 137,000 in "Wholesale & Retail Trade and Hotels and Restaurants," followed by 64,000 in "Construction."[13] These statistics reflect documented workers, so in reality, the numbers may be higher. Most Korean Chinese in the study work in "3-D" (dirty, dangerous, difficult) industries like these, which are characterized by low social status, high risk of physical and/or mental injury, and few legal protections under the law as workers. Most Korean Chinese male unskilled labor migrants with whom I speak are currently or have previously been employed in factories and assembly plants producing objects like leather goods, camping equipment, boxes, or chocolate. Others work at construction sites or interior contracting firms, though these jobs are declining in number. Of the women respondents, a majority work in restaurants, bakeries, convenience stores, bath houses (*jimjilbang*), or motels. All these jobs have high turnover rates and variable terms of employment.

The work is physically demanding. Myeong Dae, currently a worker at a chocolate factory, puts it simply: "There's no good company to work for in South Korea. Work is hard. It's dirty, hard, and difficult." Korean Chinese speak of constant body aches and joint pain associated with repetitive tasks and chronic coughing from frequent exposure to chemicals and dust. Their hands are often marked by heavy calluses as well as occasional injuries like cuts, bruises, or welts incurred on the job. In addition to these physical challenges, prolonged separation from their families exacts a high emotional cost for many Korean Chinese. In a quiet voice, Yu Na, a domestic worker who has been in Seoul for six years, says, "If I don't think about it, it's easy to forget. But at night after work, I . . . miss them [my children]. My heart hurts when I think of them."

A non-governmental organization (NGO) focused on expanding human rights for Korean Chinese and facilitating discussions about reunification is based at the church. The founder of the NGO, Reverend Seo, also serves as the main pastor of the church and leads services on most Sundays. Chul Mu works in the main office of this NGO and is one of the many Korean Chinese who entered South Korea more than ten years ago as an industrial trainee, or *yeonsusaeng*. Gregarious by nature, Chul Mu made me feel welcome at the Korean Chinese church from the first day I arrived. Wrinkles at the corners of his eyes deepen when he smiles, which is often. He tells me that in his hometown in the Yanbian Prefecture in China there are too few employment opportunities available, so many Korean Chinese move to South Korea to search for jobs. After graduating from high school, Chul Mu became one of these migrants. As a trainee, he started at an assembly plant but quickly lost his legal status when he left to look for higher-paid jobs in other companies. To pay off his debts quickly and maximize his remittances back to China, Chul Mu had little choice but to "run away . . . you have to leave without saying a word." He blamed the low wages set by South Korean companies that knew workers became undocumented if they left their sponsor. Particularly for men, undocumented status translates into longer stretches of unemployment, with very few employed at the same worksite for long, and overall very little contact with South Korean employers.

While the current visa system was reorganized in 2005, at the time of my interviews, most Korean Chinese workers entered on the D-3 "technical trainee" or the D-4 "general trainee" visas.[14] Applicants for these visas must provide a "letter of personal security assurance" to prove their financial stability as well as a recommendation from a sponsoring company. For those entering as "trainees," legal status is contingent on employment with the sponsoring company, which strategically keeps wages low. Trainee visas give greater control to employers and less mobility to workers like Korean Chinese.[15]

Both documented and undocumented trainees in manual, low-skilled/semiskilled jobs are particularly vulnerable to exploitation in the workplace. Reports of physical, emotional, and/or sexual abuse; violence; passport seizures; lack of access to unions and substandard, unsanitary working conditions without sanctioned breaks; and lower wages than their South Korean coworkers, as well as lack of overtime or holiday pay are widespread for foreign workers, including the Korean Chinese in the present study.[16] According to South Korean government estimates in 2004, more than 64 percent of the total foreign workforce in South Korea are said to be undocumented.[17] Korean Chinese comprise the highest proportion of manual workers and as such often find themselves at the center of the debate around "illegal" workers.[18] Many Korean Chinese return migrants were initially motivated by seductive stories of ample job opportunities and higher wages carried by the "Korean wind" (*hanguk baram*) in the face of underdevelopment in China. The stories do have some truth. Chul Mu explains, "You can make a year's worth of wages in China in a month in Korea. . . .

You can make 10,000,000 won[19] in a year, if you really save your money. . . . You can't make [that] in ten years in China." Across my conversations with other Korean Chinese, I heard similar estimates that one day's wages were equivalent to a month's salary in China or that a year's worth of wages could be earned in a month.

In reality, the economic benefits of labor migration to South Korea have significant downsides, particularly in terms of under-employment as well as exploitation at the hands of employers. However, the circulation of compelling stories of higher wages in South Korea serves important functions back in China. They strengthen the economic logics carried by the "Korean wind" that provide justification for long-term separation from families and communities left behind in China. They also pressure Korean Chinese to endure the hardships they face as low-skilled labor migrants in South Korea so they can return to China as success stories and in turn inspire the next generation of labor migrants.

The broad sorting process into professional and manual labor categories is one important mechanism by which labor migrants are channeled into specific occupations, which in turn, has conse-quences on the kinds of interactions they have with South Kore-ans. The other consideration is whether a return migrant is eligible for the "family" visa category.

Acknowledging or Discounting Coethnicity

Exclusive "family" visa categories institutionalize hierarchi-cal nationhood in that they are available only to certain return migrants, like Korean Americans. As one of the beneficiaries of these categories, Gloria explains, "I'm on the F-4 visa, the special gyopo[20] visa, the greatest thing in the world, that's what people tell me. . . . It doesn't tie me or bind me to any contract." Accord-ing to a 2013 survey, 124,000 F-4 "Overseas Koreans" visas were issued, though this number reflects only those who meet the qual-ifications, not necessarily all who identify as part of the Korean diaspora.[21] F-4 visa holders are given rights similar to South

Korean citizens. This translates into mobility in the job market without fear of compromising their legal status, which is not the case for trainee visa holders. However, the only migrants eligible for this visa are former *South Korean* citizens and their immediate descendants, who can validate their ethnic ancestry through the official Korean Family Census Registry known as *ho juk deung bon*.[22] Those who qualify for the F-4 visa enjoy generous privileges such as multiple entry/exit, legal work permits for two-year periods, and property ownership. Additionally, F-4 visa holders are legally prohibited from engaging in manual labor.

As was made evident in my uncomfortable exchange with the Korean Chinese men from the church at the start of the chapter, most Korean Chinese are ineligible based on that particular criterion of ancestry because their families immigrated to China before the political establishment of South and North Korea. A very small number of Korean Chinese can enter through an F-1 visa, which is for long-term visits to South Korean relatives. Applicants need to provide official documentation of their relationship with South Korean family members, including marriage and birth certificates, which are difficult to access for most Korean Chinese. As a result, both family visa options remain frustratingly out of reach for a majority of Korean Chinese.

The costs of migration are borne differently by Korean Americans and Korean Chinese, particularly in terms of how they structure their lives in Seoul. Debt incurred while moving to South Korea is a significant factor for many Korean Chinese, while not mentioned at all by Korean Americans I spoke with. The lifestyles of many Korean Chinese are defined by austerity and self-sacrifice. Yu Na, the domestic worker who has been separated from her children for six long years, says it took about two-and-a-half years to repay her debt. Because room and board comes with her job, she keeps her monthly budget around 50,000 won a month (just under US $50). This lifestyle enabled her to pay off her debt and remit the majority of her wages back to her family in China. Her situation is not uncommon. Another domestic worker, Hye Soon, who has been in Seoul for the past seven years, says that in her first year and a half, she found a live-in position and survived on 76,000 won a month (about US $70) by limiting her expenses to only essential needs. Some factory workers are very disciplined during their years in Seoul, abstaining from drinking or smoking during their leisure time, opting instead to meditate or engage in religious worship. In addition, most Korean Chinese pay a high emotional cost as a result of long-term separation from young children and spouses left behind in China. Their stories are marked by a sense of loneliness, partly ameliorated by daily phone calls and e-mails with family, bolstered by visions of a better future because of their sacrifice.

In stark contrast, these costs are nearly absent in interviews with Korean Americans. Korean American respondents are largely single and unmarried individuals in their early to late twenties, at a time in their lives when they strive for emotional and financial independence from their parents, and not financially responsible for their families back in the United States. As Gabe puts it, "the dominant group of Korean Americans . . . just graduated from college [and didn't] know what they wanted to do. They like to play, they like to be seen." Their focus is largely on the plentiful job options at relatively high wages that afford them a lifestyle outside of their reach in the United States. The annual salary for teaching English, based on the estimates I am quoted from interviews with Korean Americans working in these fields, are anywhere from US $30,000 for part-time work to over $50,000 for full-time work. Apart from those paying off student loans, none of the Korean Americans refer to migration debt or obligations to send remittances back to the United States regularly.

Unlike Korean Chinese professionals, most Korean Americans working at South Korean companies command higher wages than their South Korean counterparts. As Lydia explains, "[my coworkers] think that I'm getting their salary, but I'm not. . . . Expats usually get 20 percent [more] in salary." With his US law degree, Matt admits, his wages are higher than his South Korean coworkers because "people who can write contracts in English are in demand." While the economic incentives are an important motivating factor for coming to Seoul, being Korean and recognized as such is also important to Korean Americans and Korean Chinese on an affective level. Both groups struggle with how coethnicity operates in the labor market regardless of whether they are skilled or unskilled workers.

References to the "Korean face," "Asian face," or the use of family terms like "gyopo" and "minjok" are common, especially for Korean Americans. This is not simply about "looking" Korean. In some cases, it also refers to a powerful form of Korean cultural capital based on linguistic and cultural knowledge that make coethnic return migrants less disruptive to South Korean workplaces than more visible foreigners. But the "Korean face" affords different sets of privileges and drawbacks for Korean Americans and Korean Chinese in their respective labor markets in terms of hiring, wages, and treatment by South Korean employers.

Advantages of the "Korean Face"

Korean Americans are aware of the advantages they gain from coethnicity and US citizenship. As Peter explains, "there's a privileged position that Korean Americans have as opposed to the other dongpo from other countries." In some hagwon and private tutoring jobs, employers prefer hiring Korean Americans over other foreigners. According to Peter, "The parents love you, the kids think you're great . . . they afford you more positive characteristics than you deserve, just from that one factor alone." In fact, Peter is surprised by the open attitudes of South Koreans once they find out he is Korean American. "I've had so many people that I've ran into that just want to befriend me, . . . 'Here's my number, let's hang out.' . . . They are interested in meeting foreigners generally, but Korean Americans specifically." Peter is keenly aware that shared ancestry isn't the only factor at work. Korean Americans find coethnicity is one of the few advantages they have over White Americans. At the same time, privileges of national origin, especially for those from the United States, elevate the status of Korean Americans above other coethnic return migrants like Korean Chinese.

In terms of the manual labor market, the "Korean face" does give Korean Chinese workers a slight edge over the rising numbers of foreign laborers entering South Korea from South Asian and Southeast Asian countries like Pakistan, Bangladesh, Vietnam, and the Philippines. Their Korean cultural capital increases their employability to some degree in South Korea because communication is easier and there are fewer potential cultural and linguistic misunderstandings. However, the advantages of linguistic and cultural capital are much more limited for Korean Chinese as compared to Korean Americans. Their non-Seoul accents and out-of-date vocabulary are perceived as old-fashioned and indicative of an uneducated background by contemporary South Koreans. As a result, most Korean Chinese are seen as less intelligent "country bumpkins," suitable only for unskilled labor in modern South Korea.

Korean Chinese women with whom I speak say they are preferred over other migrants in domestic work and child caregiving because they are fluent in Korean, familiar with Korean dishes, and even celebrate the same traditional holidays. As coethnic caregivers, they can be more smoothly integrated into the family and are less jarring for children who likely spend more time in their care than with their own parents. This is true for Hye Soon, a fifty-seven-year-old domestic worker and caregiver who favors bright-red lipsticks and constantly delivers well-timed wisecracks and witty one-liners. Her present employer has two children, aged eight and four, and she says, "Besides their grandparents, I'm probably their favorite. When I'm not there, the kids cry, even the eldest. They call me 'big mom' (*keun umma*). They cry when I tell them I'm leaving, and when I arrive at their house, they get really excited." The use of family terms like "umma" (mother) by the children, presumably with the consent of their parents, signifies a level of closeness between Hye Soon and the family but certainly doesn't erase the fact that for her, ultimately, "it's a job that pays money."

Overall, for jobs that take place in the intimate context of the private home with a high degree of regular contact between employee and employer, Korean coethnicity works as an advantage for both Korean Americans and Korean Chinese. But the problem of "looking" but not "acting" Korean raises challenges, particularly for Korean Americans.

Not Korean Enough

The consequences of violating unspoken rules about workplace behavior dominate the narratives of Korean Americans but are nearly absent in those of Korean Chinese. The reason for this is that professional workers generally stay with the same employer for longer periods of time and have more regular daily contact with South Korean employers and coworkers as compared to blue-collar workers. In particular, Korean Americans in the study speak often about the ways South Korean coworkers and employers use references to "shared blood" and ancestry to reprimand and assert control over them in the workplace.

Korean language fluency (or lack thereof) is one of the main sources of tension for Korean American skilled workers. Even for those who are conversant in Korean, accurately expressing their ideas is not always a smooth process. For example, Lydia describes tension that arose from a misunderstanding with a coworker because "I had it in my head in English, but in the translation, it doesn't work out right." Some Korean American teachers deliberately sidestep this issue by avoiding situations in which they must use Korean. In some cases, they unapologetically make it clear that they are Americans. Jin Ho currently works as an English professor in a South Korean university but previously worked at a hagwon where she felt undervalued by her employers despite her master's degree in education from Northwestern. As she explains, "It is just a typical hagwon, typical Korean management; [they] treat their teachers like dirt. I'm a real teacher, I deserve some respect. . . . At work, I only speak English. Some of the office staff speak Korean, but all my colleagues are foreigners." In a workplace dominated by Americans, both ethnic and nonethnic Koreans, her strategy of asserting her educational credentials and strong American identity underscores that English is the language of power in that context. It also serves as a reminder to her employers that she sees herself as an American expatriate like her other non-Korean colleagues.

Beyond fluency in both Korean and English, Korean Americans are also expected to be aware of *how* they talk. In a hierarchical workplace culture in which rank is carefully respected, communication is strictly top-down. For Lydia, this is very different from her work experiences in the United States, where her supervisor encouraged a more collaborative way of working through disputes. In the context of her South Korean workplace, dissenting opinions about an assignment or decision are disrespectful and considered "talking back." While initially Lydia expected to have an equal voice in the workplace, she quickly learned that as a midlevel manager, "if you disagree with a superior, they get pissed off." Overall, being part of the South Korean labor force means juggling both the cultural capital associated with Americanness and Koreanness, which are often at odds with each other.

For Korean Americans in general, the pressures of conforming to local norms means adapting to the common practices in South Korean workplaces. The unexpectedly long workdays are a difficult adjustment, but for many Korean Americans, the mandatory social outings with supervisors after work are even more taxing.[23] These often revolve around heavy drinking into the early hours of the morning and become spaces in which additional problematic interactions with coworkers occur. Annie explains, "It's expected that you drink with other people to get to know them," but it also creates a situation that makes it difficult for someone, particularly in a lower position in the company, to refuse. One Korean American woman says one time she was seated deliberately across from her boss because he wanted to "look at something nice." Under his watchful eye, she poured drinks all evening for her male senior colleagues, a role traditionally assigned to women and those of junior status.

South Korean employers often invoke the term "gyopo" to pressure Korean Americans to, as John puts it, "play along with Korean rules." John works as an English teacher at an exclusive high school where "the administration expect Korean Americans to teach like a foreigner but understand Korean things. 'You're Korean, we have the same blood.'" Although the school hires a number of foreigners who are not ethnically Korean, John feels that South Korean employers treat Korean Americans differently "because we look Korean." The phrasing emphasizes the important distinction between "looking Korean" and "being Korean" for Korean American workers, a nuance not generally acknowledged by South Korean employers.

In some cases, the pressure to fit into the South Korean workplace means being pressured to go along with "a lot of shady stuff," as Lydia put it. Lydia was brought to South Korea as a consultant since she had worked in a US branch of the same company. She noticed that her South Korean employers engaged in "creative bookkeeping" practices that fell outside the company's guidelines. For example, in monthly reports, she discovered that her managers "would hide a certain amount. In the next month, if they didn't get to their budget level, they put that there." Lydia knows "you can't have things hidden here and there," but this is something commonly done in South Korea. For Catherine, questionable practices are routine within the South Korean work culture, particularly for men. She notes the common practice in her company for her male coworkers to go out to "room salons" after business dinners with (male) clients.[24] Korean American respondents tend to see these "shady" practices as exclusive to Korean businesses, despite ample evidence of corruption, fraud, and under-the-table antics by US corporations and prominent American businessmen.[25]

Nate is a Korean American who at one point overstayed the limit on his tourist visa while working for a hagwon. His undocumented status did not phase his employers, who just "paid for me to go in and out [of the country]." Nate enjoyed a quick trip to

Hawai'i to reset his tourist visa thus regaining his legal status, as least for a few months. Although he benefits from these actions, Nate is well aware that his "employers encouraged the illegal." But like Lydia, he goes along with questionable actions, chalking it up to the way business is done in South Korea. Following the rules also means adapting to a "Korean ethic" of "just putting in the time." Korean Americans I spoke with share numerous stories about South Korean coworkers playing online games, watching soap operas, or even sleeping at their desks without consequences. In a workplace with an accepted "lackadaisical" work culture, Korean Americans are concerned about a promotion system that is solely based on hours spent at the desk and in the office, as well as seniority in the company.

In their critiques of South Korean work practices, Korean Americans tend to idealize the meritocratic nature of US workplaces. The compelling yet inaccurate narrative of the "American Dream," based on "pulling yourself up by your bootstraps," features prominently in Korean American understandings of perceived injustices in their work experiences. For example, in explaining the difference between the United States and South Korean work culture, Lydia believes that in the United States, "at least if you work hard, you show it, you go up." But in South Korea, "you can do all the hard work you want or you can do nothing, and in ten years, you'll be at the same level." I hear this over and over in comments like "you're keeping long hours even if you're doing shit at work" and "you can do jack-shit for 10 years; you'll get a high paying salary later" and "as long as you sit there, you're showing your solidarity or commitment to the company." While the United States ties success to individual merit, South Korea is seen as more antiquated, valuing quantity of time spent at one's desk over the quality of one's work.

It is unsurprising that most Korean American workers do not anticipate long-term, permanent employment in South Korea and are well-aware that, as Jessica puts it, "I have the experience they want to have. I have a specific role. Once they get the information they need, my job is probably gone." The decision to hire a foreigner outside of the system is pragmatic and ends when their South Korean employers acquire the knowledge and skills they need.

Too Korean to Be American

While Korean American professional workers undeniably benefit in concrete economic and social terms as Americans, they struggle in South Korea with a *racial* logic that makes them too Korean to be "real" Americans and a *cultural* logic that makes them too American to be Korean. In fact, the label "American" is used by both Korean Americans and South Koreans in reference to Whites. In the English-teaching and college prep industries, some Korean Americans feel a "weird reverse discrimination" in hiring practices—a thinly veiled preference for Whites by some Korean employers. Korean Americans watch with resentment as White Americans find employment more quickly than they do, leaving racial preference for Whites as the only explanation. Chun Ja, a Korean American woman who moved to Seoul with her White American partner, Mike, notes a distinct difference in their experiences in the job market. As she explains, "Everyone is fawning over Mike. He got so many job offers. For the first month, I don't get anything. . . . There are certain hagwons that will not hire anyone with an Asian face."

For Korean American workers, this means developing concrete strategies in response to situations when their Koreanness undermines their Americanness. Maya, a Korean American woman who works in the English voice-over industry, tells me about an employer who fired her on the spot when he found out she was Korean American. Maya was furious that he was "so obvious" about his desires for a "real" American, someone visibly foreign, not a Korean American. To hide her Korean American identity from prospective employers in the entertainment industry, Maya says, "I don't want to put my photo on anybody's website. I don't want anybody to see that I am a gyopo. Because when I speak, I sound like a White girl." Maya's strategy is to accept White as the de facto standard of true Americanness by doing what she can to mask her racial and ethnic identity and speaking "like a White girl."

Hye Weon shared a similar story of being "mistaken for Korean" when looking for a job in the English-teaching industry. After a successful phone interview, Hye Weon arrived at the offices to find a dramatic shift in tone when they saw her in person. She says she was told, "'[because] you're a gyopo, you're on a[n] F-4 visa, we can't hire you as a foreigner.'" But it is clear to Hye Weon that those employers had a racial preference for "a straight-up White person. They [South Koreans] don't like darker skins either." The conflation of whiteness with Americanness as well as the pressure to act "Korean" in the workforce places Korean Americans in a double bind in which they are either "too Korean" to be American or "not Korean enough."

Hierarchical Nationhood in the Skilled Labor Market

These kinds of struggles within South Korean workplace culture, such as not being seen as foreign enough or being forced to socialize with employers and coworkers, are generally absent in the narratives of Korean Chinese. This can be attributed to several factors. First, their concentration in blue-collar industries offers very little contact with South Korean employers, and their coworkers in these jobs are often other foreign migrant workers. Also, the physically demanding nature of their jobs means very little down time for socializing, which keeps interactions at a minimum in general. Additionally, many Korean Chinese often work on day-to-day contracts, not staying with the same employer long enough to develop the kinds of personal relationships that Korean American workers do.

In addition to labor migrants, I meet Korean Chinese graduate students at the church who attend my English classes regularly, one of whom is the head of a Seoul-wide Korean Chinese student association and has a large social network composed of other Korean Chinese education migrants and professional workers. Through him, I meet Hye Yong who works at the Korean

Advanced Institute of Science and Technology (KAIST), a well-respected research university, after finishing her master's degree in China. Unlike Matt, the Korean American lawyer introduced earlier in the chapter who earns more than his South Korean colleagues, Hye Yong notes that "even though I am better educated, as a foreigner, I can't command the same wages as South Koreans." While her coworkers are polite and helpful, she is aware that they do not see her as Korean, only as Chinese. In fact, Hye Yong tells me a South Korean coworker once joked that if she spoke in Japanese (Hye Yong is fluent in Japanese), she would be perceived in a more favorable light because she could "pass" as Japanese. Despite working at the institute for the past year, Hye Yong has formed few close relationships with coworkers, rarely attending social gatherings outside of work. This differs significantly from the experiences of Korean Americans working in South Korean firms, who generally report receiving higher salaries relative to their South Korean coworkers and being invited, even pressured, by colleagues to attend social functions.

Unlike Korean Americans, Korean Chinese like Hye Yong do not possess *unique* linguistic, educational, and social capital seen as desirable to South Koreans, such as degrees from internationally prestigious universities or native English fluency. Her engineering degree does not distinguish her from her South Korean coworkers, so there is no justification for a higher salary. This differs from Korean American professionals whose Ivy League (or equivalent) credentials and fluency enable companies to present a more global presence in industries. As a result, Korean Americans are afforded a great degree of control over their work situations, particularly compared to Korean Chinese. On the whole, their US citizenship, American cultural capital, and credentials alongside their Korean ancestry translate into class privileges and elevated social status in Seoul. The disparities between Korean Americans and Korean Chinese in the workplace seem to support Hye Yong's assertion that "the country you come from makes a difference." For Korean Chinese, the fact that China is their country of origin has a noticeable effect on even small interactions, such as this one

Kyeong Won describes that took place when she was employed at an export–import firm in China. She had worked with a South Korean businessman for an extended period of time. For their last meeting, he brought a cosmetics set from South Korea as a thank-you gift. When Kyeong Won arrived in Seoul, she tells me with a laugh, "I saw Missha [a Korean cosmetic brand] . . . and I was so offended! What is that man thinking, bringing such a cheap gift when he is wealthy!" For her, the low value of the gift did not reflect the level of respect she feels she deserved. Instead, she sees it as evidence of the general level of condescension South Koreans display toward Chinese—the businessman assumed she would not recognize the cheap quality of the product.

For Kyeong Won, Hye Yong, and other Korean Chinese workers, it is not just the negative perceptions and treatment of Korean Chinese in general but the raised status of other diasporic Koreans like Korean Americans that is truly unfair. Kyeong Won notes, South Koreans are more deferential to "people who are better than them, [have] more money than them. They respect and want to be like them. But for people they think are lower than them, don't live as well, they treat them as inferiors." Rather than utilizing and valuing them for their ties to a powerful ally in the Asia region, South Koreans are largely dismissive of Korean Chinese, seeing them solely as blue-collar, low-status workers even when they are white-collar professionals who possess substantial work experience and advanced educational degrees.

Unskilled and Exploitable: Korean Chinese Manual Workers

Although educated and skilled Korean Chinese professionals do migrate to South Korea, second-generation Korean Chinese in the study generally arrive as unskilled blue-collar workers. As noted in the previous chapter, many come from Yanbian Prefecture and were raised in strong ethnic Korean immigrant communities where they attended officially sanctioned Korean Chinese schools. Unlike third-generation Korean Chinese, second-generation Korean Chinese in the study say they are more comfortable speaking in Korean than Chinese and have much lower levels of educational attainment. Because of higher levels of Korean cultural capital, geographic proximity, and job opportunities, South Korea is a favored destination for many Korean Chinese unskilled labor migrants.

Family terms like "dongpo" or "gyopo," which are regularly used by South Korean employers in reference to professional Korean American workers, are largely absent in the narratives of Korean Chinese blue-collar workers. Korean coethnicity, to the extent it is mentioned, is used to extract more labor out of their employees. For example, Yu Na explains, "Korean Chinese are seen as better for housework than South Koreans. Since we don't have a home, our own families, or place to go . . . we can stay twenty-four hours and do everything." She went on to say, "they [South Korean employers] prefer us also because they can pay us less than South Korean workers."

Most Korean Chinese unskilled manual laborers or service workers work under flexible, unstable contracts with no health insurance, getting paid below minimum wage or without compensation for overtime hours. Given the chronic unemployment experienced by many Korean Chinese I meet, there is much less detail in their stories about interactions with specific South Korean coworkers and employers as compared to Korean Americans because they do not have established relationships with them. For the most part, Korean Chinese are vague when discussing their employers, perhaps because of high turnover rates but also their understandable reticence to talk to me as an outsider to their community.

Child Caregivers and Domestic Workers

The Korean Chinese domestic workers in the study are an exception. They share stories that are rich in detail often because the nature of the job put them in close daily contact with their employers within the intimate sphere of the home. In some cases, they work for the same middle to upper-middle class South Korean families for years. Social scientists have studied the ways gender, race, ethnicity, and nationality shape the unequal power relationships present in this industry, which centers on already undervalued reproductive labor relegated to the "women's sphere."[26] These inequalities are particularly visible in Western countries in Europe and the United States, where a majority of the work relationships are between White, middle and upper-middle class women from postindustrialized countries and non-White women (im)migrants from developing countries.

However, in the case of Korean Chinese domestic workers employed by South Koreans, these same gender and class inequalities are replicated even though employers and employees share the same ethnic identities. In these relationships, nationality becomes a powerful marker that trumps coethnic ties and widens the social and economic distance between coethnic citizens of semiperipheral and peripheral countries. Korean Chinese women are also set apart from the "respectability" of educated middle-class South Korean women, who either work outside of the home or are freed from the "dirty" aspects of household. These workers are made more vulnerable because the workplace is in the private sphere, removed from the public, and largely unregulated.

Yu Na has worked as a caregiver and domestic worker for a number of families during her years in Seoul. She is a slender forty-six-year-old woman with a soft voice. During our interview, especially when discussing more serious topics, Yu Na avoids eye contact, fixing her gaze at her hands folded on the table in front of her. She does this when describing one of the worst employers she had. "For no reason at all, they would work me to death. They would tell me that I'd have to clean things with a rag instead of a vacuum, and make me crawl into every corner to clean the beds, make me wash clothes even though they'd only worn it once." Her voice trails to a near whisper, "They treated me like I was a slave or something."

Hye Soon estimates she has worked as a domestic worker for over ten different employers during her seven years in Seoul. While never subjected to physical abuse, in one case, Hye Soon says her South Korean employer "kept me in like a prisoner." Stories of employers withholding pay and keeping their passports are common among Korean Chinese domestic workers. Additionally, tending to the needs of young children is a twenty-four-hour responsibility, so there is often little time to themselves "off the clock." Being treated as a "prisoner" or "slave" is insulting because it goes against their belief that South Koreans and members of the Korean diaspora are part of the same "race" (minjok) and should be treated with respect and dignity. The absence of the language of family and references to shared blood, so commonly reported by Korean Americans, allow South Korean employers to distance themselves from the exploitative nature of the job and the workers who do it.

Like domestic workers, Korean Chinese factory workers also say they receive lower wages and are often assigned more physically demanding tasks than their South Korean coworkers. Interestingly, Korean Chinese workers, perhaps because of their ambiguous status as ethnic Koreans and foreigners, are largely absent from the history of Korea's strong labor movement around foreign migrant workers' rights in 3-D industries.[27] While construction work, assembly work, domestic work, and child care are undeniably hard, these conditions are compounded by social discrimination and negative perceptions of Korean Chinese in South Korea. This is unexpected for some Korean Chinese workers like Chun Hwa who had thought that "South Koreans were just like me" and assumed a closeness based on these kinship ties. But instead, she finds, "they treat us like *oegukin*"—foreigners—"not dongpo." In the end, it is an advantageous situation for South Korean employers who can *extract* as much labor as possible at the lowest cost.

Undocumented Workers

The growing number of undocumented workers within the Korean Chinese community because of violations of the narrow restrictions of their visa categories contributes to their negative reputations in South Korea. Their undocumented status is a bitter pill for Korean Chinese to swallow because it denies any acknowledgement of their coethnic ties and shared histories with South Koreans. From Chul Mu's point of view, part of the problem is this: "They [South Koreans] view us as . . . uneducated and unskilled. They will use us for labor since they don't have enough people willing to do those jobs. . . . If we really are part of the same family [minjok], then South Koreans should help Korean Chinese live better lives." This same sentiment is echoed by Kwang Soo, who notes that "by cracking down on illegal immigrants, South Korea is enforcing international and domestic policies that are making laughingstocks of people who are still their brothers."

The exploitative treatment of Korean Chinese as compared to the elevated status of Korean Americans is seen as unfair since both communities can equally trace their ancestry back to the Korean peninsula. A third-generation Korean Chinese who had been working in various South Korean factories for three years, Myeong Dae sees it like this: "Since America is good, and since South Korea views America as the best, American dongpo are all looked upon with favor. . . . South Koreans think Japan is better than South Korea. If you can speak a little English and Japanese, then they favor those dongpo as well." After a moment of silence, he sighs and says, "They just see me as a Chinese man." Yet being seen as a "Chinese man" is not wholly accurate. Myeong Dae's statement speaks to the ways in which "Chinese," a category that includes Korean Chinese, is equated with cheap, expendable labor in the eyes of South Korean employers. The label has become a shorthand way to refer to Myeong Dae's low social and economic status as a manual worker as well as an erasure of his emotional connections to South Korea as a homeland.

"I Deserve Some Respect": Strategies of Resistance

To gain respect as workers, Korean Americans and Korean Chinese rely on two different economic strategies with respect to their identities as "family" or "foreign" using the language of happenstance. While Korean Americans in the study enjoy relatively privileged positions within South Korean immigration policies as well as the labor market, they push for recognition that they are first and foremost Americans whose ethnic identities "happen to" be Korean. In so doing, they solidify their economic positions by choosing to downplay their Koreanness and emphasize their Americanness. This strategy has two important implications. First, Korean Americans do not challenge the disparities created in the diaspora by hierarchical nationalism in South Korea by renouncing their access to the F-4 visa, "the greatest thing in the world," in solidarity with Korean Chinese and others excluded from it. Their privileged status does not require them to. Second, Korean Americans do not challenge assumptions of whiteness as ideal Americanness. Instead, they assert they are just as American as Whites and should be treated as such. If South Koreans know they are not "Korean Korean," then Korean Americans, like other foreigners, should not be expected to speak Korean fluently or act like Koreans.[28]

In contrast, many Korean Chinese continue to express a strong sense of pride in their ethnic Korean ancestry. The longing to be recognized and treated as family offers an alternative to the dehumanization they experience as workers. Particularly for manual laborers, respect as workers is important because it allows them to frame the abuses they endure as violations of their rights as workers. They work in physically grueling conditions and make many personal sacrifices for a better future, including years of separation from young children for the betterment of their family. Simply put, Korean Chinese want an end to dishonest practices by South Korean employers and want to be treated as human beings with shared ancestry and histories, rather than economic units. Kyeong Won expresses a common refrain of Korean Chinese in South Korea: "Of dongpo, there are the most Korean Chinese, but they have the fewest rights."

It is clear in repeated comments such as "Our blood is the same" and "Joseon is our home," and references to "minjok" that many Korean Chinese identify as part of the broader Korean family.[29] The language of family deliberately uses *affective logics* to argue that all members of the Korean diaspora deserve the same level of respect. As such, Korean Chinese argue that they should be treated in the same way as all other dongpo regardless of their countries of origin and the kinds of jobs they do. To this end, some Korean Chinese frame their Chinese nationality as a matter of happenstance. For example, Ok Hwa says, "Korean Americans, their grandparents or parents went to the US, Korean Japanese went to Japan, we [Korean Chinese] went to China. . . . But Korean Chinese are from poor areas in China, so even though China is getting wealthier, South Koreans think they can ignore Korean Chinese." Because they lack the agency to hold individual employers accountable, Korean Chinese focus their attention on the unequal visa system as the root of their problem in Seoul because it has deep social and economic repercussions in their lives. Being reclassified by South Korean institutions as "family" can make a tangible difference in terms of their own structural position in South Korea.

Inclusion in the Korean family implies a strong sense of obligation between coethnic return migrants and South Koreans. It means that pejorative attitudes by South Koreans and abusive treatment at the hands of employers are inexcusable. It also comes with the expectation that South Koreans have a responsibility to help their family, especially when they are struggling. For example, many Korean Chinese point to their own efforts back in China to support North Korean refugees who cross the Tumen River seeking asylum. They put their own lives at risk because North Koreans, like anyone tied to the Korean peninsula, are minjok—"family." As a second-generation Korean Chinese man explains, "If we are relatives . . . and you came from South Korea to China, we would give you food until literally the legs of the table would break, even if we can't afford it." But he has found that South Koreans are "not as generous . . . and do not treat us respectfully like honored guests." Through legal status as family, Korean Chinese can separate themselves from other foreigners doing unskilled labor and access the same concrete benefits and respect as dongpo that are granted to Korean Americans and Korean Japanese.

Conclusion

The juxtaposition of the work narratives of Korean Americans and Korean Chinese reveals the impact of hierarchical nationhood on the daily lives of return migrants and its material consequences. The hierarchical *vertical* structure for South Korean nationhood entrenches social, economic, and legal disparities by stacking more fortunate members of the diaspora, like Korean Americans, above Korean Chinese. Paradoxically, despite strong discrimination stemming from their low social and economic status, most Korean Chinese display a greater attachment to their Koreanness as a strategy to increase their rights in South Korea and maximize their economic potential as *legal* workers *and* legitimate members of the Korean family. Many Korean Chinese, especially second-generation manual laborers, push for a more inclusive *horizontal* framework of diasporic membership in which *all* dongpo can access the same privileges, regardless of nation of origin.

For Korean Americans, acceptance of the advantages of *vertical* diasporic membership means they perpetuate unequal relationships under hierarchical nationhood. By asserting their Americanness, Korean Americans go one step further by seeking a place outside of the South Korean nation, freeing themselves from the baggage of the "family" category and associating themselves more closely with visible foreigners like White Americans. Their strategic responses highlight the agency of return migrant workers, who are not passive recipients of the labels imposed on them by South Korean immigration policies and South Korean coworkers and employers. Their engagement with and against the hierarchies speaks to the tension between opposing frameworks—vertical and horizontal—of Koreanness.

3

Of "Kings" and "Lepers"

*The Gendered Logics of Koreanness in
the Social Lives of Korean Americans*

My god, there are Koreans everywhere. It's amazing! . . .
Everyone I saw on the street looked like someone back home . . .
It is really odd. They looked familiar, [and that is] sort of
comforting. . . . In the States, I'm Korean, I'm Asian, and then
I'm a guy. In Korea, I'm just a guy. The only level of difference is
the fact that I'm American. Something about blending in that
I'm not used to. . . . It's nice, wow, kind of cool just feeling
like I'm everyone else but, at the same time, totally different.

On the surface, Adam's comment seems to state the obvious. It
should come as no surprise that Koreans would be everywhere in
South Korea. Adam realizes that in South Korea, he could shed
a lifetime of marginality as a racial minority in the United States
and claim membership as part of the dominant racial group. But
this moment is a passing one. But the longer Adam lives in Seoul,
the more he realizes, "You're kind of on the outside . . . on the
periphery, because you're not really Korean." As a Korean

American, Adam is not "Korean Korean" and, as such, finds himself positioned on the outside in both positive and negative ways.

The previous chapter discussed how Korean Americans and Korean Chinese are structurally positioned as "Korean, but not really Korean" in the eyes of South Korean immigration policies and the labor market, though in very different ways. In the next two chapters, I shift the attention from institutions to the interpersonal dynamics of social relationships. Departing from previous research on return migration, which has largely focused on the tension between ethnicity and nationality, the juxtaposition of Korean Chinese and Korean American narratives evidences the ways ethnicity and nationality intersect with other axes of difference. The discussion highlights the unevenness of transnational identities both across and within each community, and the potentially exploitative and one-sided nature of diasporic belonging.

In this chapter, I examine how Korean Americans see gender as the lens through which they experience the greatest challenges to their ethnic identities as Koreans. Why is it that most Korean American return migrants with whom I speak believe that Korean American men live like "kings" in Seoul, while women are relegated to a status below "lepers"? How do they respond to these differences in social positions? To answer these questions, I discuss the various cultural and economic logics used by Korean Americans to make sense of the normative expectations around femininities and masculinities in South Korea. Based on their overall assumption that the United States "does gender" better than South Korea, Korean Americans develop strategies to maximize their social status as foreigners in relation to South Koreans. Notably, men and women accomplish this through distinctive gender strategies.

Gender Strategies as "a Plan of Action"

According to sociologist Arlie Hochschild, a "gender strategy" refers to "a plan of action through which a person tries to solve problems at hand, given the cultural notions of gender at play."[1] She examines gender strategies in the context of how married couples divide the labor of the daily, weekly, and monthly chores—such as cooking, cleaning, and child care—that keep households functioning smoothly. Hochschild finds these decisions are not based solely on the desires of each individual actor but are shaped by broader ideas about femininity and masculinity. Unpaid work, often referred to as "reproductive labor," within the home is largely delegated to wives based on cultural assumptions that women are "naturally" more nurturing. In contrast, "productive labor," or paid labor outside the home, is the duty of men who are generally assumed to be the economic providers. Interestingly, even with changing trends in labor force participation and shifting ideas about femininity and masculinity as a result of the women's movement of the 1960s and 1970s, Hochschild concludes the gender strategies around reproductive labor often conform to these deep-rooted cultural norms.[2]

In my study, I extend Hochschild's concepts by examining what happens when "gender strategies" are further complicated by ideas around ethnicity and nationality. As a result of return migration, how do certain "cultural notions of gender at play" produce conflicting cultural expectations about desirable "Korean" femininities and masculinities? And how do they impact the social interactions and intimate relationships between South Korean and Korean American women and men? I focus on the ways Korean Americans in South Korea employ various gender strategies rooted in economic and moral arguments to accomplish two goals. One is to maximize their social status, particularly in the heterosexual dating market for single actors and within blended South Korean–Korean American households for married individuals. The second is to push back against attacks by South Koreans to their legitimacy as "real" Koreans because of their failure to conform to dominant notions of femininity and masculinity. The gender strategies of Korean American women and men appeal to the interaction effect of their national and ethnic ties, ultimately strengthening their identities as *Korean Americans* rather than South Koreans. However, as a result of competing strategies, Korean American women and men are generally unsympathetic to the perspectives of the other gender, highlighting fissures within the community itself along gendered lines.

Marginalized Asian American Masculinities in the United States

"Korean American guys in [the] US, they get totally emasculated. In [South] Korea, it's a hyper masculine society. Korean American guys get all the benefits from it. As a Korean guy, you're mainstream. The benefits of speaking English, you're from the US—you're kind of special." This is how Nate describes his perspective of what it is like to be a Korean American man in Seoul. The narratives of Korean American men in the study, like Nate, are peppered with frequent references to the "emasculation of Asian American men" in the United States, particularly their perceived social undesirability and invisibility. Rather than viewing masculinity as simply rooted in biological factors, gender scholars have long argued that masculinities are historically and socially constructed.[3] In the United States, the type of masculinity with the greatest amount of social and economic privilege, referred to as "hegemonic masculinity," is almost exclusively associated with wealthy White heterosexual men. While hegemonic masculinity represents a set of unattainable ideals, it remains a powerful set of cultural beliefs that legitimate certain kinds of masculinity as dominant while subordinating and marginalizing others based on hierarchies of race, sexuality, and class.[4]

For Asian American men, the tangible realities of "hegemonic masculinity" are often visible in their dating lives. Most Korean American male respondents were frustrated with their social lives in the United States, especially in comparison to White heterosexual men. For Gary, his "0 percent success" rate with women growing up in a predominantly White neighborhood in New Jersey meant that he felt socially invisible and undesirable. Adding insult to injury, many men shared numerous examples of getting rejected by Korean American and other Asian American women only to see those women go on to date White men. Many men attributed this to the weak, generally negative representations (if represented at all) of Asian American men in US popular culture. The experiences of Korean American respondents in the US exemplify the power of what sociologist Patricia Hill Collins calls "controlling images" in mass media.[5] These images shape expectations around heterosexual dating norms and the ways Asian American men are excluded from successful masculinities therein.

"Controlling images" refers to specific stereotyped images, particularly of African Americans, "designed to make racism, sexism, and poverty appear to be natural, normal, and an inevitable part of everyday life."[6] Extending this to depictions of Asian Americans, Yen Le Espiritu traces a similar history of racist and sexist portrayals by cultural institutions that "help justify the economic exploitation and social oppression of Asian American men and women over time."[7] For example, the evil mastermind character Fu Manchu epitomizes the notion of Asians as the "Yellow Peril." His slanted eyes, generic "Oriental" clothing, and a characteristic wispy, long mustache highlight a vague, sinister "Asianness." Closely related to this controlling image is the stereotype of Asians as "unassimilable foreigners" who can never achieve true Americanness even if they have lived in the United States for generations. Socially, there is also a long history of the undesirable Asian American man in American culture. For example, consider the sexually charged, nerdy foreign-exchange student, Long Duk Dong, in the 1980s John Hughes film "Sixteen Candles." His awkward interactions with his host family and heavily accented and flawed English as well as the stereotypical gong noise that accompanies his on screen appearances are constant reminders that Long Duk Dong is Asian, foreign, and falls well short of normative expectations around American masculinity. It is a foregone conclusion that the protagonist (Samantha, played by Molly Ringwald) will end up romantically with Jake, the handsome, wealthy White jock. The character of Long Duk Dong is solely seen as a comedic foil, rather than a true romantic rival.

These highly constrained controlling images of Asian American men are powerful because of their remarkable consistency over time. Even today, there are very few, if any, shows or movies that cast an Asian American in a leading role.[8] They remain type-cast as sidekicks, awkward businessmen, geeks, nerds, accountants, and engineers who may be economically successful, even funny, but rarely the object of romantic or sexual desire. The effect on the American popular imagination is that of a symbolically cas-trated, undesirable, and frequently overlooked Asian American masculinity.

The impact of cultural images is not restricted to the screen; it has a tangible effect on the identity construction and social relationships of Asian American men. Coined by psychologists, Alexander Lu and Y. Joel Wong, the "minority masculinity stress theory" outlines the particular stressors on the mental health of Asian American men.[9] Their findings suggest that Asian Ameri-can men struggle with the pressures of the unattainable hegemonic masculine gender roles, which are compounded by the added stress of the model minority image. The negative impacts of marginal-ized masculinities are not solely psychological but also social and economic. In some cases, Asian American men internalize the very stereotypes they tried to challenge.[10] These struggles are evident for the Korean American heterosexual men with whom I speak. They refer often to the negative characterizations of Asian men in the United States, including being comparatively shorter in stature, less athletic, less popular, less physically endowed, and less imposing than White men and other men of color. The cumulative effect is that they feel dismissed as effeminate or assumed to be gay, weak, awkward, nerdy, and desexualized, none of the qualities associated with the ideals of a desirable, virile, romantic partner.[11] However, these narratives change significantly as a result of return migration and the shifts in social status and gendered experiences of Korean Americans in South Korea.

"We Live like Kings": Gender Strategies of Korean American Men and Global Hegemonic Bargains

While the marginalization of Asian men in the United States has been well studied in academic research, there has been little examination of masculinities in a global framework, particularly in a context in which Asian American and Asian masculinities collide. A focus on gender in South Korea, where Asians constitute the majority group, highlights the shifts in meanings of desirable masculinities and femininities among members who share ethnic ties. In South Korea, the advantages of coethnicity combined with US cultural capital translates generally into a boost in status for Korean Americans in Seoul. As Adam explains, "There's a sense of empowerment just because you're a man, you're a gyopo, you speak English. You fit in; race isn't an issue here." This impression is common among Korean American men, evidenced in comments like "I can totally milk the hierarchy here," "In Korea, for a male, you can basically do whatever the hell you want," and "Just bring out your passports; you'll have girls all over you."

While Jim is clearly frustrated when talking about the social experiences of Asian American men in the United States, he becomes much more animated when discussing the way gender, socioeconomic class, nationality, and race operate in the context of South Korea: "You come to Korea, an Asian American man, . . . it's not what it [was] before, but Asian American men are pretty near the top. First of all, they are a novelty. Second of all, they have money. Even working in a hagwon,[12] you are making more than the normal man. The way you spend is more than a rich Korean. You're way up there at the top." The rise in their social status in Seoul comes up repeatedly in conversations with other Korean American men who talk about it in terms of a "reversal of fortune" or as "black-and-white different" from their experiences back in the United States. They "live like kings" by embracing markers of hegemonic masculinity that elude them as Asian American men.

In the context of hegemonic masculinity, social scientists have argued that men marginalized in one social context often display more extreme forms of masculinity to exert power over others in their communities. In so doing, men displace their anger from discrimination and exclusion from the dominant group by exercising their power over women and other more marginalized groups of men in their own communities.[13] Sociologist Anthony Chen found a similar dynamic when looking at the dynamics between two groups of marginalized men in the United States: Asian Americans and immigrant Asians. He argued that Chinese American men enacted a "hegemonic bargain" to elevate their status in relation to immigrant Chinese men by "consciously trading on, or unconsciously benefiting from, the privileges afforded by their race, gender, class, generation, and/or sexuality."[14] Applying this within the context of return migration from the United States to South Korea, I argue Korean American men make a "global hegemonic bargain" by strategically using their combination of ethnicity, nationality, and economic capital to benefit from US privilege and patriarchy and to align themselves to the ideals of hegemonic masculinity. Few Korean American men actively challenge the benefits that they receive. In fact, most actively assert their American privilege to claim greater social, sexual, and economic power over South Korean men and women, as well as Korean American women.

BECOMING "SEXUAL COMMODITIES": VISIBLY SUCCESSFUL HETEROSEXUALITY

Sae Il critically observes, "There's a change of fate. In America, Korean American men are castrated, . . . they're humiliated, they're not 'real men.' All of a sudden, Korean American men come to Korea, [and] they're a sexual commodity." Many Korean American men in the study talk about South Korean women as tools to enhance their masculinity, often through boasts about their sexual exploits and social desirability.

Perhaps the most graphic example of this is a private e-mail sent by Peter Chung, a young Korean American man working at an international investment firm in South Korea that went public and triggered a controversy in both South Korea and the United States:

I've got a spanking brand new 2000 sq. foot 3 bedroom apt. with
a 200 sq. foot terrace running the entire length of my apartment
with a view overlooking Korea's main river and nightline. . . .
Why do I need 3 bedrooms? Good question, . . . the main
bedroom is for my queen size bed, . . . where CHUNG is going
to fuck every hot chick in Korea over the next 2 years (5 down,
1,000,000,000 left to go). . . . I go out to Korea's finest clubs, bars
and lounges pretty much every other night on the weekdays and
everyday on the weekends [. . .] I know I was a stud in NYC
but I pretty much get about, on average, 5–8 phone numbers a
night and at least 3 hot chicks that say that they want to go home
with me every night I go out.[15]

His message puts on display a hypermasculinity buoyed by the
economic and social benefits he accrues as a Korean American
heterosexual man. Demeaning language referring to women as a
"harem of chickies" or "hot chicks" is paired with an aggressive
heterosexuality evidenced by Chung's attempts to quantify his
sexual desirability by the number of girls he can "fuck" at the end
of the night. Capped off by descriptions of his luxurious, expensive apartment and a decadent lifestyle filled with clubs, bars,
and lounges, I argue Chung's message embodies elements of the
global hegemonic bargain used by Korean American "kings" to
elevate their status in South Korea as Asian American men. Sexist
remarks and references to wealth in the Chung e-mail can be read
as an attempt to distance himself from the emasculated, invisible
status of Asian American men in the United States.

While none of the Korean American men in the study use
Peter's extreme language, there are some strong parallels between
their gender stories and his. For example, while making clear that
he is faithful to his girlfriend back home, Gary sheepishly admits
that "a lot of Korean American guys come out here to hook up
with a lot of Korean girls." Jim states this more bluntly. From his
perspective, "getting with" lots of attractive South Korean women
is "the number one reason why Korean American men are out
here." The idea of "easier" South Korean girls and the opportunity

to become "sexual commodities" in South Korea is a welcome change from their years of pent-up social and sexual repression as marginalized Asian American men in the United States. Rather than attributing it to a dramatic change in their personalities or appearances, many Korean American men recognize that their popularity is built on the "novelty" of being Korean American, or *jemi* gyopo.[16]

CLASS PRIVILEGE AND KOREAN AMERICAN LAVISH LIFESTYLES

Korean American masculinities are often tied to displays of financial privilege as Americans. As mostly young, single, childless adults with no dependents back home, some Korean Americans men in the study refer to their wages as "play money," "spending money," or "monopoly money" because they are not sending remittances. Other expenses such as housing and even amenities like cable and cell phone plans are sometimes provided for them by their employers. For example, as an English teacher, Nate has an arrangement with his hagwon that gives him a subsidized, furnished apartment along with his hourly wage.

Economic privilege is one way in which Korean American men claim a position of power over South Korean men. As Jim explains, "Even working in a hagwon, you are making more than the normal [South Korean] man. . . . Most gyopos, we live like kings. [We] do things that [South] Koreans won't even imagine doing. . . . like going to nightclubs, going to drink wine, spending $100 in one night." He admits, "It hurts us financially, . . . but for [South Koreans], that's a once a year thing, it'd be this special occasion." He ends by saying, "Here, if I don't go out, what do I do?" dismissing the many cultural opportunities in the metropolis of Seoul and emphasizing the particular life stage a majority of my Korean American respondents are in. When asked about why they initially moved to South Korea, most Korean Americans stated culturally centered goals such as learning Korean and getting in touch with their Korean roots. However, the longer they are in Seoul, their unspoken goals as single, heterosexual men appear to shift toward earning money and having an active social life.

Another strategy of the Korean American global patriarchal bargain is to trade consciously on the privileges of being an American to portray themselves as "better than" South Korean men. Many Korean American men in the study criticize South Korean masculinity as damaged, characterized by heavy drinking, adultery, and being physically and mentally abusive and neglectful of their family duties. This is particularly true for Craig, a Korean American adoptee. Initially, he returned to South Korea in search of his biological parents, placing advertisements in major newspapers and scouring his files from the adoption agency for any information that could help him locate them. While his investigation was ultimately inconclusive, he says the move to South Korea "made me realize what my adoption issues are. I hate Korean men." He starts laughing and counting on his fingers beginning with his thumb, "Here we go. They drink, they smoke, they cheat on their wives, they stay out late . . . they neglect their children . . . pretty much everything I [don't] want to become."

Despite the fact that Craig has lived in South Korea for three years and has a South Korean fiancée, he refuses to learn more than the very basics of the Korean language because "I don't want to be seen as a Korean man." Like Craig, many Korean American men distance themselves from a flawed South Korean masculinity as a gender strategy that is devised across ethnic and national identities. Even though they engage in many of the same behaviors—such as excessive drinking, smoking, and staying out late—as single young South Korean men, Korean American men see their lifestyle as acceptable because they are neither cheating on their wives nor neglecting their children.[17]

But there are passive benefits to a stigmatized South Korean masculinity for Korean American men as well. As Craig explains, "I know if I blow my top, lose my temper. . . . in [South] Korea, it would be pretty normal [because] . . . it's not uncommon for a [South] Korean male to blow his temper and bitch someone out." He is quick to say, "In America, I would never do that . . . it would be totally absurd," but in Seoul, "I know that I can get away with it . . . because of my size and because [I'm] a man." The global patriarchal bargain means that Korean American gender strategies allow them the flexibility to disparage or align themselves with South Korean masculinities depending on the context to maximize their social status while in South Korea.

"OVERCOMPENSATING MEGALOMANIA": CRITIQUES OF KOREAN AMERICAN HYPERMASCULINITY

South Korean men are not the only targets of contempt. Some Korean American men are highly critical of their peers. For example, Sae Il, a thirty-year-old mixed-race Korean American, says that the newfound social popularity and disposable income "completely goes to their head. It manifests itself in this form of overcompensating megalomania, which I can't stand to be around." Sae Il links the "megalomania" of Korean American masculinity to the powerless position of Asian American men in the United States, concluding, "They're just thinking about basically how they can benefit from a situation that's really unequal." Craig feels similarly frustrated by Korean American men, "I got so sick of their bullshit. . . . Korean Americans coming over in the summer, with more money than they know what to do with, and pissing their life away. . . . [All] they talk about [are] girls, cars, and money."

Although both Craig and Sae Il are critical of Korean American men and their expressions of hypermasculinity, they continue to experience individual social and economic benefits based on broader structural privileges accorded to Americans in South Korea. As a native English speaker with a college degree from a prestigious university, Craig's privilege allows him to make the choice of learning Korean or not. Additionally, as a multiracial individual with a South Korean immigrant mother and a White American father, Sae Il is quick to criticize "those Amerasians from the US [who] can play the role of the White boy, the foreigner, and have access to all sorts of white privilege here in Korea."[18] It should be noted that even as he emphatically refuses it, Sae Il's biracial appearance may actually grant him white privilege in Seoul.

"Don't Take This the Wrong Way . . . Korean American Women Have These Weird Problems"

The last aspect of the global hegemonic bargain is exercising dominance over women. The relationships of Korean American men with South Korean women discussed earlier, defined by quantity rather than quality, are often used, at times crudely, as a form of control. They also boost their status by marginalizing Korean American women, often making negative assumptions about their reasons for coming to South Korea. Or more simply, they accept that, as Nate puts it, "girls get the short end of the stick here." There is general agreement that Korean American women are seen, albeit unfairly, by South Korean men as "slutty girls" because of their Westernized identities. Jim explains, "Korean men would much rather date a Korean woman because Korean American women are a little bit too independent . . . Even Asian American men don't want to meet Asian American women, because they can just meet them at home. Even White women are above Korean American women, because they're the novelty. There's no novelty in a Korean American woman." While Korean American men are more than happy to benefit from their US status and wealth, they seem to accept that Korean American women are penalized for these same qualities.

But rather than sympathizing with the plight of Korean American women, Jim feels most "Korean American men think that Korean American women are—don't take this the wrong way—there's something wrong with them. . . . Why would you go from here to here"—he gestures from high to low—"on the totem pole? [Maybe] they stole their best friend's boyfriend, their boyfriend is trying to kill them . . . drug problems, money problems." From Jim's perspective, "there's no viable reason for Korean American women to come out here," which highlights the primary importance he places on social status. The reference to the "high" position of Korean American women on the totem pole in the United States reveals the ways that Jim feels Asian American women benefit from the exoticization and eroticization of

Asian American women in the United States. After a lifetime of marginalization in the United States, Korean American men like Nate and Jim protect their newfound social status in South Korea by normalizing Korean American women's subordinate status and enacting extreme forms of masculinity to claim power over South Korean men and women.

"... So Lepers Are above Us?": Subordinated Korean American Femininities

Paula is a twenty-four-year-old who initially arrived as part of a Fulbright program after graduating from college. After finishing her contract, Paula stayed on in South Korea and has been here for the past three years. Her maturity is evident throughout our interview, particularly in the deliberate silences she takes before answering tricky questions and the thoughtful way she chooses her words. Her perception of the social hierarchy in South Korea is consistent with many other Korean Americans in the study, especially women. As she explains, "Top is White males, then Korean American males, then Korean m[e]n, then White female[s], then there's everyone else in between, then at the bottom, Korean women, then lepers, and then it's Korean American women. . . . I was like, 'So lepers are above us?'" In terms of the heterosexual dating market, Paula feels Korean American women are not socially desirable to prospective partners: "[It's] because we're so individualistic—or too aggressive, or whatever—we're not seen as very good women. . . . No man wants to marry us; we're too headstrong."

Korean American women attribute their stigmatized social status to the generally undesirable characteristics commonly ascribed to them by South Koreans. Some critiques include being "too dark skinned," "too assertive," "too aggressive," "too independent," "too loud," "rude," "too headstrong," "too educated," "openly blunt," and in general, unattractive. Given these stereotypes, it is unsurprising that Korean American women in the study negatively assess the gender climate in Seoul in comments like, "Korea is horrible for Korean American girls," "[Korean American women] are just loud, obnoxious and fat," and "When I am in a Korean environment, . . . I'm more subdued and shy; I'm not as confident of myself." On the whole, Korean American women see the critiques of their physical appearance and behaviors by South Koreans as constant reminders that they fail to meet normative ideas of South Korean femininity. Part of the problem is the outdated framework that Korean American women use to characterize the role of women in South Korean society that automatically positions them as adversaries to South Korean women.

CONSTRAINED SOUTH KOREAN WOMEN, LIBERATED KOREAN AMERICAN WOMEN

Pointing to deep-rooted Confucian ideologies, Korean American women see limited options for South Korean women beyond narrow roles as daughters, wives, and mothers. For some Korean American women, this message comes from frustrating interactions with their South Korean relatives. Despite her many professional and educational accomplishments, including the Fulbright fellowship, Paula feels her South Korean relatives only understand her in three roles, "I'm my mother's daughter, I'm my husband's wife, I'm my child's mother—I'm nothing else." As an unmarried working woman with her own apartment, Paula concludes, "I don't have a role in this society."

Paula is not alone in this type of thinking. Chun Ja is another Korean American woman who similarly describes the constrained roles available to South Korean women. "As a woman, unless we want to live like the totally conventional Korean life where we have an arranged marriage and live here as a Korean housewife for the rest of our lives, there's not much for us here other than making money for a short period of time." The implication is that the only option for South Korean women is to be assigned their partners and become housewives, while Korean American women can aspire to be working professionals outside the home and aim for "love marriages" rather than arranged ones. In addition, women are expected to raise the children, clean the home, and cook meals, while men are the sole breadwinners. While inaccurate, these assumptions support a gender strategy that enables Korean American women to claim proud identities as *American* professional women who are not constrained by what they see as traditional roles for Korean women.

Working women married to South Korean husbands in this study provide interesting insights into the varying gender strategies available to Korean American women depending on their position in South Korean society. For example, Jennifer's in-laws live with her and her husband, following Korean tradition in which parents generally go to live with the eldest son. As a result, Jennifer feels both subtle and direct pressures from her South Korean relatives to be more group- or family-oriented and more submissive. Even though Jennifer works long hours as a financial consultant, she finds herself taking on more of the reproductive work in the home because of her mother-in-law's presence. As she explains, "If it was just my husband and I, I would ask him to do dishes more, help around the house more. But . . . it makes me look bad when I ask him to do things, so sometimes I have to accept the fact that often I have to do more than my share, per se, because I don't want it to look like I'm not a dutiful wife."

The uneven division of labor is most apparent during traditional holidays like seolnal or chuseok[19] when families often gather in celebration and women assume most, if not all, of the preparation duties. Jennifer remembers her frustration in the days leading up to chuseok, when "women are wearing aprons in the kitchen working, cooking for two days" and taking care of the children, while men are largely not expected to do anything. We share a laugh because I encountered a similar situation when I spent chuseok with my South Korean relatives. I was conscripted to peel and chop endless piles of vegetables while my uncles and male cousin lounged in the living room, seemingly oblivious to the mayhem in the crowded kitchen. Jennifer says, "When I first entered the family, I always found myself at least one of the three days of the holiday crying, upset about the injustice of gender roles." Her frustrations deepen because the unequal division of labor is widely accepted by the other women in the family, including her four sisters-in-law and her mother-in-law.

After enduring years of this "injustice," Jennifer says she held an "intervention" with her extended family to restructure the delegation of some tasks associated with the holidays in a more equitable way. Her primary message was that "in the West, men do contribute to the family as well," implying that the US ideologies about gender are more egalitarian. While she acknowledges that "there is a part of me that wants to respect the wishes of my mother- and father-in-law, there is a limit to how far I'll go." Jennifer was pleased that the following year: "My husband and some of his brothers helped with the dishes. Five years [later], the men are now [completely] responsible for the dishes." Notably, the successful redistribution of duties and the assumption that men in the West help in the home is based on a narrative that American heterosexual households are gender-progressive spaces in which labor is evenly divided between men and women—a myth thoroughly debunked by Arlie Hochschild.[20] In addition to struggling under the perception that South Korean women's value is only in the reproductive realm, Korean American working women find the pressures of behaving like a proper Korean woman to be an extremely frustrating part of their economic lives in Seoul.

"IT'S A MAN'S WORLD": GENDER AND PATRIARCHY AT WORK

"It's hard enough being a woman here because it's still a man's world," Catherine says matter-of-factly. According to a recent study released by the Organization for Economic Cooperation and Development (OECD), South Korea is ranked the lowest among the thirty-four member nations in terms of the employment rate of women with college degrees. At the same time, South Korea is in the top ten among OECD countries in terms of educational attainment, with over two-thirds of twenty-five- to thirty-four-year-olds completing postsecondary school degrees. These statistics suggest that while South Koreans are one of the most educated populations in the world, women college graduates remain underemployed or leave the workforce at higher rates than similarly educated men. In this context, it is perhaps unsurprising that Catherine feels that rampant gender inequality and sexism in the workplace make South Korea a hostile environment for women.

Sexist attitudes become evident early in the interviewing process. For example, Jessica remembers being asked particular questions: "[Employers asked] if I had babies, am I planning to have babies, would this affect my abilities to work, how much money [I made at my previous job], my age." With a sigh, Jessica continues, "No matter how many trainings they have about this, they can't turn it off. . . . It is bizarre. They wanted to know how I treated my mother and father, whether I embody a lot of . . . Korean characteristics." Annie believes that while American women might balk at these kinds of questions, "[South Korean] women accept that once they're past twenty-five, they're less hirable. If they're married, they're less hirable."[21] While many Korean American women share comparable stories, none of the men I spoke with say they are asked to discuss their commitment to their family or plans to have children. Limiting this line of questioning to prospective women candidates reveals an underlying assumption that family duties would interfere with only women's abilities to work, one that is not limited to South Korean employers. But in the narrative of Korean Americans, it serves the purpose of supporting a belief system that the United States is more gender egalitarian and forward-thinking than South Korea—something I return to later in the chapter.

Once hired, Korean American women struggle with gender-segregated workplaces. Korean American professionals working in South Korean firms in the study say most, if not all, other women in the workplace are in secretarial and other support staff roles. For example, as the only female and foreign manager in her office, Lydia often feels out of place and even ignored by her South Korean male coworkers. As she explains, "When you look at management here, they are all guys. There are only two supervisors that are girls. It's very segregated." She continues, "In the beginning when they had management meetings, they never called me." Rather than seeing these actions as deliberately spiteful, Lydia believes they forget to include her because her coworkers are unused to the presence of women in meetings. After voicing her frustrations to her supervisors about being left out of key decisions or conversations, she now attends regular management meetings. However, her coworkers often admonish her for being "too loud" and "too aggressive"—characteristics they perceive as "too American" and outside the boundaries of proper Korean femininity. In addition to the limited representation of women in the workplace, the sexist and patriarchal standards applied to them are points of contention. Catherine says, "Even my guy friends that work at these firms, they tell me, . . . 'We definitely ask for pictures. We only hire hot girls'—and these are big firms like Samsung." She interprets this practice to mean that the value of women workers in South Korea is tied to their physical attractiveness, rather than professional skills, a situation that she incorrectly believes does not occur in the United States.

For Korean American women, the combination of looking *and* talking like a South Korean means further pressures to conform to the rules of normative Korean femininity. Even though Catherine was hired as a teacher explicitly because she is a native English speaker, there is still the expectation as a Korean American that she should be fluent in Korean. As she puts it, "If you don't speak Korean fluently in the workforce then . . . they [South Korean coworkers] look down at you. 'Oh you should, because you are Korean by blood, why don't you speak it fluently?'" But it is a catch-22, because, as Catherine explains, "if you are fluent, they expect you to act like a subservient, submissive Korean girl." The disadvantage of the "Korean face" is that Korean American women are subject to restrictions in ways that White American women are not. Catherine believes because they are visibly foreign, "White women . . . can put [their] foot down, be a bitch, and nobody will say anything. 'Oh she's American.'" Unlike Korean American women, White women can confront Korean patriarchy without censure because they are clearly foreign.

Like Catherine, most Korean American women rely heavily on an overly simplified and fixed characterization of the work cultures of both the United States and South Korea. Korean American women use cultural arguments based on a vague notion of "Korean tradition" to criticize the sexism entrenched in South Korean workplaces but absent in American ones. As Lydia explains, "Korea and Japan are the most traditional. . . . When all the world is progressing, if [South] Korea and Japan regress, sooner or later, we're going to fall behind." Rather than individualized to a few employers or coworkers, sexism is seen as a deep-rooted characteristic of South Korean culture.

In contrast, Korean American women depict US workplaces as more gender progressive and modern than South Korean workplaces. Citing the increasing visibility of American women as well as people of color in positions of economic, social, and political power, most Korean Americans dismiss the "glass ceiling" and the "bamboo ceiling" as relics of the past. Part of this can be attributed to their economic status in the United States as young, highly educated, mostly middle- to upper-middle-class individuals, which may have shielded them from many of the challenges related to racism and sexism as workers. While Annie does acknowledge that gender inequality continues to be a problem in the United States, she points out that "we [Americans] do have [anti]-discrimination laws. You can't ask a woman if she's pregnant; you can't ask for a picture."

By framing what is "American" and "Korean" as oppositional and hierarchical concepts, Korean American women in the study replicate the findings of Karen Pyke and Denise Johnson, who find that Asian American women generally see "ethnic realms" as sites of gender oppression and patriarchy, whereas "mainstream settings," read as White, are sites of gender equity.[22] The respondents in their study feel more constrained because of cultural pressures in Korean or Vietnamese spaces and believe they are their more authentic selves in "American" spaces. Similarly, Korean American women I speak with generally see the United States as more gender progressive and "better than" South Korea. For them, "mainstream" is still rooted in the United States, and Korean cultural traditions and ideologies are repeatedly seen as the root causes of the oppression of women in South Korea. There are two unintended consequences of this gender strategy. First, patriarchy, racism, and sexism embedded in the United States go critically unexamined, ignoring the research by feminist scholars of persistent gender inequalities in the United States such as the wage gap, the glass ceiling, increased sexual and physical violence against women, and the "time bind" resulting from the unequal division of reproductive labor in the home.[23] Second, the overgeneralization overlooks the important social transformations in South Korea in the past few decades, such as the dramatic increase of women in the labor market; a vibrant, active feminist movement; and rising divorce rates and higher numbers of single-parent homes that challenge the assumption that South Korean women are all housewives in nuclear families.

By characterizing South Korean culture as sexist and immutable, Korean Americans make little mention of the unconscious and conscious ways they benefit from privileges linked to their US citizenship and Westernized cultural capital. Instead they replicate the "West is the best" ideology based on an idealization of US culture as more gender-egalitarian than patriarchal. That said, the prevalence of similar stories in interviews speaks to the very real challenges of sexism and patriarchy in the everyday lives of Korean American women in South Korea. As is the case in their interactions with South Korean employers and coworkers detailed in the previous chapter, Korean American women feel they are unfairly expected to "act" appropriately according to local norms rather than treated as foreigners because they "look" Korean. In response, Korean American women develop gender strategies that dismiss the social popularity of Korean American men as a temporary phenomenon and position themselves as different from and better than South Korean women.

Chun Ja contextualizes the newfound desirability of Korean American men in South Korea in relation to the marginalized status of Asian American men in the United States. As she puts it, "It's hard to be seen as a macho man when there is no real concept of an Asian American man being sexy or cool in America." But she is quick to point out that while Korean American men "would be total losers and dorks" in the United States, in South Korea, "they're like players."[24] Korean American women resent the fact that US citizenship and shared Korean ethnicity work against them even as these same factors elevate the social desirability of Korean men. As Paula explains, "Korean American men are *jjang*, the best of the best. They speak English and Korean, they're American born, they have that access to America. . . . They [South Korean families] want to marry their daughters off to them; they see them as a success. Their parents went over, are able to produce this great son that's coming back to [South] Korea and [is] rediscovering his roots. . . . Oh perfect, perfect, perfect"—she claps her hands—"Korean American women are like"—she makes a disgusted sound.

The reputation of Korean American men is in stark contrast to the social experiences of Korean American women, whose identities as Americans and ethnic Koreans become a source of their marginalization. As Catherine explains, "I don't like that Korean American guys can . . . be nothing back at home and be kings out here, and Korean American girls have to go the other way around." While it successfully put these "players" in their place, this gender strategy does little to challenge the marginalization of Asian American men in the United States.

"BAD" SOUTH KOREAN WOMEN AND "GOOD" KOREAN AMERICAN WOMEN

The most prominent gender strategy used by Korean American women rests on the construction of South Korean women as "bad" or "weak" women. In large part, this comes in the form of critiques of their physical appearance and behaviors as "pale," "extremely thin," "anorexic," and "homogenous." Korean American women denigrate South Korean women for policing their own bodies to achieve a homogenous image of beauty and valuing the importance of physical appearance over other more substantive qualities, such as intellect and ambition. While Hye Weon concedes that "Korean Korean girls are much prettier than Korean American girls," she attributes it to "the superficiality of trying to keep up with everyone."[25]

Age does not seem to grant immunity to the pressures of performing appropriate femininity. Sixty-one-year-old Sandra, the oldest participant in the study, was born and raised in South Korea and then attended a US boarding school for high school. Sandra went on to graduate from a US college, marry a White American man, become a US citizen, and work in an import–export business for the past twenty years. She returned to Seoul indefinitely for family reasons, but no longer feels "Korean Korean" after so many decades away. Sandra rejects the constant negative comments from her friends and family members about her appearance: "Mostly clothing, hair, makeup, all the superficial things which I have a total disregard for. I just can't put up with that." But not all Korean American women dismiss these family pressures. Since marrying a South Korean, Jennifer says she finds herself paying more attention to her appearance after been told explicitly by her relatives that "you should take better care of your makeup, your hair" because in South Korea, "when a woman goes out in public, it's a matter of being proper."

Korean American women point to the homogenized features of many South Korean celebrities who use plastic surgery to "Westernize" their faces, from double-eyelid surgeries to other adjustments to make eyes appear larger and wider, nose bridges seem narrower and raised, and chins look sharper and more defined. The abundance of plastic surgery clinics in Seoul and the profusion of "lightening" and "whitening" skin products on the market speak to the broad popularity of a particularly desirable look that is more Western than Korean. Many Korean American women share funny stories about what they see as the excessive techniques of South Korean women to protect their skin from sun damage. These include sunscreen products with impossibly high levels of SPFs, parasols, gloves, arm sleeves, and the ubiquitous shaded visors, which one woman refers to as the "Darth Vader mask," that fold down to obscure one's face completely. It is not just about how South Korean women look but also their behaviors themselves. Korean American women take issue with *aegyo*, a set of behaviors almost exclusively directed at men marked by a high-pitched, wheedling tone with elongated vowels, accompanied by stomping feet and shaking shoulders. Korean American women interpret *aegyo* as a form of manipulation by South Korean women to get men to provide for their needs while acting in an immature childlike manner that plays up masculinity as a more powerful status.

Korean American women manage their subordinated gender identity by criticizing South Korean women, distancing themselves socially, and seeing their own behaviors as a matter of choice. For example, if a Korean American woman does not wear makeup, it is because she is more confident and less concerned with the judgment of others. However, if she does wear makeup, she does not do it in the homogenous style of South Korean women, who "pancake" their faces with concealer and foundation to achieve the "perfect" complexion. Another example is that many South Korean women live at home until marriage. For Korean Americans, this is interpreted as a sign of a lack of independence, whereas in fact this decision may have been out of financial necessity rather than choice. Korean American women tend to discount their access to relatively high-waged, plentiful jobs by virtue of their US cultural capital. Overall, Korean American women have little sense of solidarity with their South Korean "sisters" despite facing similar challenges of sexism and patriarchy in the home and at work. As a gender strategy, many Korean American women choose to emphasize the differences between themselves and South Korean women, whom they generally dismiss as complicit in their own oppression and trapped by a traditional culture that imposes highly constrained roles for women. Along with negative assessments of their appearance, *aegyo*, their materialism and "obsession" with brand names, Korean American women are particularly critical of the sexual behaviors and attitudes of South Korean women.

"I'VE SEEN SOME OF THOSE GIRLS AND THEY'RE RAUNCHY": REGULATING THROUGH SEXUALITY

I return to Lydia, whose frustrations at work are detailed earlier in this chapter. She is an animated speaker, expressive with her body language as well as her words, throwing up her hands to punctuate points from time to time. When it comes to her opinions about dating in South Korea, she does not hold back:

> Korean native girls, they're blunt but very submissive in front of guys. They're so two-faced. . . . I think guys have fun because Korean girls are easy. . . . They say that Korean girls are hos. In Korea, they're either really nice or they're not. Korean girls are very conniving too. . . . Us gyopo [Korean American] girls are more conservative than the girls here, because I've seen some of those girls and they're raunchy. . . . My guy friends would tell me all these stories. At clubs, they can randomly have sex with two girls. . . . My guy friends have done it—why would they lie?

Lydia, like most Korean American women with whom I speak, has very few, if any, South Korean women in her social networks, which allows her to categorize them as a homogenous group. For most Korean American women respondents, their main contact with South Korean women is at work, where they tend to have minimal interactions, or socially as the girlfriends of Korean American men. Although she jokingly says that she is "boy crazy," Lydia finds that men, both Korean American and South Korean, tend to avoid Korean American women. She thinks this is because in South Korea, Korean American women are presumed to be promiscuous because of their Western upbringing and the fact that many live alone and not under the direct supervision of their families. But from Lydia's point of view, the reality is reversed. Her use of terms like "two-faced," "hos," "conniving," and "raunchy" suggests that the popularity of South Korean women with men, especially Korean American men, is because they are willing to "put out" in ways that Korean American women do not. In so doing, Lydia uses moral arguments to position Korean American femininities as different from and better than South Korean femininities.

Like Lydia, Veronica hates the double standard in South Korea that elevates Korean American men into "players" and relegates Korean American women to a status "lower than lepers." "I really need this today," Veronica says as we sit down at a restaurant for *jook*, a comforting rice porridge well suited for rainy, cold days. Veronica is really angry because she was fired recently from her hagwon because of her "attitude problem" and is still fighting her former employers for her last paycheck. When the conversation turns to her thoughts on the social scene in Seoul, she laughs and shakes her head. The last time she came to Seoul was in college, over ten years ago. Her ex-boyfriend attended the same program, and she definitely remembered the differences in their experiences. "He came, he had a blast. . . . He was the hot shit, the Korean American gyopo. He is tall, good-looking, perfect, great, all the Korean girls were after him. I was struggling—'Oh I have no rights in Korea'— I'm dealing with that stuff. . . . I left and was so happy to be back in America. He extended his initial six months to a year. The whole treatment by society is different. Korean American males are the hot ticket for Korean girls to immigrate and get out." Lydia and Veronica engage in a similar gender strategy by portraying South Korean society as inherently patriarchal and South Korean women as "conniving" because they see dating Korean American men as a "ticket" to move to the United States.

Constructing South Korean women as "bad" or "weak" is problematic for a number of reasons. First, it facilitates the ideological "buy-in" of Korean American women to the hierarchical relationship between the United States and South Korea. Korean American women equate the United States with progress and development and see South Korea as socially and economically backward. They hold on to this belief even with clear evidence that contemporary South Korea, especially Seoul, is highly developed and modernized.

Second, Korean American women's gender strategies engage in "slut shaming," a set of discourses that uses moral arguments and conservative ideas about femininity and sexuality to regulate and castigate so-called loose promiscuous women. This is evident in their criticisms of South Korean women, which range from allegations of "too many" casual sexual partners to the idea that they dress and act in a sexually provocative manner to manipulate Korean American and South Korean men. Additionally, Korean American women generally dismiss South Korean women as "just" housewives, rather than career women. By using traditional ideas about sexuality and femininity to judge and position themselves as superior to South Korean women, these gender strategies leave patriarchy unquestioned.

NOT TOO AMERICAN, NOT TOO KOREAN

"Maybe I don't see the sexist stuff as much except for the marriage thing. . . . I have more under my belt. I have a master's degree; I can make money in Korea. What they see as deficient is my marital status; they can't give me shit about much else." Almost unconsciously, Veronica straightens up when she says this. Her goal in South Korea is to use her skills to save up as much money as possible before she returns to the United States. Her identity as a professional teacher is her armor against what she feels is the judgment of South Koreans toward her as an unmarried Korean American woman in her late twenties. Veronica and many other Korean American women I speak with realize they can never "pass" as South Korean women, even if they try. As Connie puts it, their Americanness is evident from "the way we dress, the way we walk." Korean American women often use intentional displays of their unapologetically American identities to mark them as "different from" and "better than" South Korean women.

A particular example is deliberately choosing to smoke out-side on the street. In fact, many Korean American women say they have been targeted by comments or stares, even being spit at in one case, for smoking outside. While permissible for men, this is generally considered taboo for women, particularly those who "look" Korean. Most South Korean women avoid censure by confining smoking to designated indoor areas such as coffee shops.[26] As Connie explains, "People stare at me whenever I have a cigarette outside. I don't know why they have to be so judgmental about it because if [South Koreans] know I'm not really Korean, [they would know] I'm not trying to be rude." By engaging in a typically masculine behavior in a public setting, Connie is asserting her difference as an *American woman* who is "not really Korean" despite her physical appearance.

Another way is to use English deliberately whenever possible. This can include a refusal to learn Korean, acquire beyond a beginner's grasp of the language, or even fake not understanding Korean to escape the constraints of traditional Korean femininity. Heather provides an example of this. She and her husband, both Korean American adoptees, came to South Korea to find their respective biological parents. While she eventually stopped searching for her parents, Heather has decided to stay on in Seoul, where she has been for the past year. As an English teacher, Heather has a job that does not require her to speak Korean, and she has no plans to improve her language skills during her time in Seoul. She justifies this decision, saying, "I have a resistance to learning Korean. . . . because once I start speaking Korean, then I have to start acting Korean. . . . There are expectations of me to act in Korean ways and I don't want to." While she says she feels "in terms of blood and heritage . . . [on] some sort of fundamental level, I'm Korean," Heather says she is "very comfortable just being an American and being treated as an American." It is important to note that the lifestyles and behaviors of these Korean American women are facilitated greatly by the economic, social benefits, and status of US cultural capital in South Korea.

As someone who identifies as Korean American, Heather likes that she is "not all one or the other. It's not like I'm having to choose one over the other." The idea of choice is compelling when faced with a stigmatized social status in South Korea, but it is also problematic. In so doing, Heather and many other Korean American women in the study align themselves with the status with the most power—in this context, as Americans, while at the same time not "that" kind of (White) American woman who is a "feminazi who is all 'women's rights' or whatever." Rather than being seen as radical gender rebels, most Korean American women strive for the same social and economic privileges conferred to their Korean American male counterparts, and they do so by upholding the subordination of South Korean women.

Conclusion

Overall the general consensus from the interviews is that in Seoul, Korean American men enjoy a dramatic increase in social status, while Korean American women experience an abrupt decline in status. In this context, Korean American men use *economic* and *cultural* arguments to position themselves as "better than" South Korean men because of their higher-wage-earning potential and supposedly more progressive gender ideologies as Americans. After a lifetime of emasculation and lack of social power in the United States, many feel justified in enjoying their social desirability in a largely uncritical manner. On the other hand, Korean American women routinely feel unjustly penalized for violating South Korean gender norms. In response, many construct a "bad woman–good woman" dichotomy using *economic, moral,* and *cultural* arguments to position themselves as "better than" South Korean women both because of their identities as professional women and their abilities to regulate their sexual behaviors and physical appearance in a more deliberate manner.

Gender stories often reveal strong assumptions by most Korean American women and men that sexism and patriarchy are ingrained, immutable aspects of South Korean culture and absent in American society. For example, Adam believes that in South Korea, "If you're a guy, you'll be treated like a god. If you're a White guy, you'll be treated definitely like a god. Women are treated like shit." After a brief pause, he concludes, "What I'm trying to say is basically acknowledging the sexism that exists here." Racial and gender logics "travel" with Korean Americans from the United States and their return migration projects only reaffirm the notion of the United States as "better than" South Korea. But gender politics do not cross borders. For Korean American men, their "global hegemonic bargain" means accepting the privileges of patriarchy and Americanness in South Korea that enables them to live like "kings" but doesn't change their continued emasculation and marginalization as Asian American men back in the United States. For Korean American women, their "bargain" allows them to use their US privilege to access high-wage jobs and become economically more self-reliant. Unlike these "poor" South Korean women, they can ultimately "escape" Korean patriarchy by returning to the United States to have a better, more liberated future for themselves as American women. The disparate experiences of Korean American women and men in South Korea highlight the need to expand the discussion of patriarchy to include different groups of men and women and between different ideas about masculinities and femininities. Axes of difference based on nationality, class, and gender fracture communities into fixed binaries, pitting Korean American men against South Korean men, Korean American women against South Korean women, and ultimately, "kings" against "lepers."

4

"Aren't We All the People of Joseon?"

*Claiming Ethnic Inclusion
through History and Culture*

As our conversation turns to the relationship between South Koreans and Korean Chinese, Kyeong Won gestures at two points on the table between us and slashes through them with her finger, "Joseon was divided into North and South Korea after the war." As her finger traces a wide circle on the table, she asks, "Aren't we all Joseonjok?" Introduced in chapter 2, Kyeong Won is a thirty-seven-year-old Korean Chinese woman who works for a South Korean company in the export–import industry. Although she is a college graduate engaged in white-collar work, Kyeong Won has experienced the contempt many South Koreans show toward Korean Chinese as social and economic inferiors. This disdain comes through in news stories that focus on the threat undocumented workers, like some Korean Chinese, present to South Korean society as potential criminals. The coverage highlights their illegality and their foreign status without any discussion of their shared coethnicity or the biases within an immigration system that favors return migrants like Korean Americans over Korean Chinese. The privilege of Westerners is evident in the value South Koreans ascribe to English and US educational credentials and the lack of prestige given to Chinese and degrees from Chinese institutions. It is visible in the ways Korean Chinese accents and vocabulary are seen as less sophisticated than the Seoul dialect.

Kyeong Won's use of "Joseon" is important. A term used commonly by both Korean Chinese and North Koreans in reference to the Korean peninsula, "Joseon" evokes a sense of Koreanness that is historically rooted rather than geographically bounded. The roots of Joseon stretch back to the Joseon dynasty, which lasted for hundreds of years, before the establishment of North and South Korea. "*Jok*" translates in English to "family," "people," or "nation." Taken together, "Joseonjok," literally means the "ethnic family, people, or nation of Joseon" with a strong emphasis on shared ancestry. By asking "Aren't we all Joseonjok?" Kyeong Won positions Joseonjok, or Korean Chinese, as the possessors of an "original," less corrupted Koreanness that supersedes the modern concept of nations and citizenship, since their existence dates back to an undivided Korean peninsula. In this chapter, I focus on the ways Korean Chinese in the study use *historical* logics to push for greater privileges, including *legal* status as dongpo in South Korea—a status already granted to two other return migrant communities. The first are Korean Americans, who are eligible for the F-4 "gyopo" visa, as discussed in chapter 2. The unexpected second reference group are North Korean "defectors," who qualify for South Korean citizenship as political migrants. In both cases, authentic Koreanness becomes a malleable cultural argument to challenge a hegemonic South Korean nationalist project in which Korean Chinese are cast as national outsiders and inferior coethnics.

Teasing apart Ethnicity, "Race," and Nation within South Korean Nationalism

The question of whether South Koreans, North Koreans, and all members of the Korean diaspora are universally accepted as members of the same "family" is a complicated one, especially since the peninsula has been divided since 1945. Part of the issue is that "race, ethnicity and nation are all conflated in Korea and this is reflected in the multiple uses of the term minjok, the most widely used term for 'nation' but which as easily refers to *ethnie* or race."[1] Blood and ancestry become the "essence" of determining one's inclusion in the South Korean nation. Based on a survey of South Korean citizens conducted in 2000, Gi-Wook Shin found that over 90 percent of respondents believed that the Korean nation had "a single bloodline" and that close to 75 percent thought that "Koreans are all brothers and sisters regardless of residence or ideology."[2] The inclusion of *ideology* in the question implies that North and South Koreans remain "family" despite deep political differences between the two nations. While this suggests a broad, inclusive approach to nationalism in South Korea, the Korean Chinese experience clearly reveals the disconnect between Koreanness as an abstract unifying concept and the divisive way it operates in reality. Even among respondents, there is no consensus about whether South Koreans and Korean Chinese should be seen as part of the same minjok.

Song Lim, a third-generation Korean Chinese man in his early twenties, offers one side of the debate. When I ask him if Korean Chinese should be included as part of the category "minjok," he shakes his head vehemently, and crosses his hands at the wrist forming an "x" in front of his body. For him, the discourse of minjok is a deliberate strategy by South Koreans to position themselves as gatekeepers for determining the boundaries of inclusion and exclusion with respect to the Korean nation. From his perspective, Korean Chinese should not try to gain acceptance into a narrow Korean identity as defined by South Koreans but instead make the category more inclusive. The constant reference to Joseon by most Korean Chinese subverts the assumption of South Korea as the core of the Korean family, by using a particular *historical* era to root the common origin for all Koreans—North Koreans, South Koreans, Korean Chinese, Korean Americans, and any other overseas Korean communities.

There is precedent for thinking about the Korean nation as historically determined, not geographically bounded. Shin Chae-ho, a prominent Korean historian and independence activist in the early 1900s, argued Koreans on the peninsula and ethnic Koreans in Manchuria were part of the same "race."[3] In the contemporary context, rather than eschewing minjok completely as a South Korean construct, other Korean Chinese in the study think of it as a useful linguistic reminder that reinforces "family" ties between Korean Chinese and North *and* South Koreans. Myeong Dae is an example of someone who holds this belief. He is a thirty-one-year-old third-generation Korean Chinese man who grew up in a majority ethnic Han town near China's border with Russia. In his eyes, "South Koreans, North Koreans, and Korean Chinese, we all use the same alphabet and everything . . . we are one family; we are all minjok." Song Lim and Myeong Dae illustrate the difficulties in locating Korean Chinese within South Korean concepts of race, ethnicity, and nationhood. However, what is clear is that nation of origin matters greatly and that Korean coethnics with Chinese citizenship are at a disadvantage in South Korea.

As discussed in chapter 2, previous research on return migration has shown that "hierarchical nationhood" is a common pattern in diaspora–homeland relations. Certain members of a diaspora often experience preferential treatment in the ancestral homeland, particularly if they are from economically and politically more powerful nations. For example, anthropologists Joshua Roth and Takeyuki Tsuda separately found that Japanese Brazilians labor migrants experienced social discrimination in Japan in part because of the negative perception of Brazil as a developing "third world" nation and the fact that they were largely employed in manual labor.[4] While the Korean Chinese experience in South Korea bears some similarities to that of Japanese Brazilians and other previous research on return migration, there are two important distinctions that make it unique.

First, homeland–diaspora relations in the Korean context are complicated because of the division of the "homeland" into two distinct nation-states with competing claims over sovereignty. Bloodlines and ancestry alone are not sufficient "natural" criteria to determine who is "inside" and who is "outside" the boundaries of Koreanness. Second, the timing of emigration takes on added importance. Unlike Korean Americans in the study who have a more straightforward identification with South Korea as the homeland, Korean Chinese orient themselves to both South and North Korea. In fact, as will be discussed later in this chapter, many have had stronger, more sustained contact with North Korean relatives and greater affective ties to North Korea. When hierarchical nationalism and the *historical* dimensions of transnationalism intersect with current geopolitics on the Korean peninsula, Korean Chinese argue they rightfully deserve the same benefits extended to Korean Americans and North Koreans as equal members of the Korean diaspora.

Strategies to Improve the Status of Korean Chinese in South Korea

Korean Chinese use several strategies to better their lives given the amount of social discrimination they face in contemporary South Korea. One option is to prove "family" connections to South Korea to attain citizenship. The Korean Chinese church where I offer English classes sustains an active campaign on behalf of Korean Chinese in South Korea to increase pathways to citizenship as well as access to the F-4 visa for return migrants.[5] Sung Bae is one of the few Korean Chinese in the study who has taken this path. He is a second-generation Korean Chinese man in his midfifties whose family immigrated in the mid-1940s to Yanbian Prefecture in China. Although born in China, Sung Bae attended Korean Chinese schools and was raised with a strong Korean identity in part because, he says, "[my] family left behind one of my siblings in South Korea and my mother always talked about South Korea, . . Joseon is our homeland." After immigrating to South Korea, Sung Bae, his Korean Chinese wife, and their two children became citizens in 2001. While he says, "I now think of myself as South Korean," citizenship does not seem to erase the social and cultural divisions between himself and native-born South Koreans. For example, his social networks remain almost exclusively Korean Chinese, and he spends much of his leisure time at this Korean Chinese church rather than a South Korean one. Additionally, his economic prospects have not increased much despite legal status. Citizenship does not change the fact that jobs in the manufacturing and construction industries are decreasing steadily, and without a college diploma or extensive South Korean networks, there are few other jobs for which Sung Bae is qualified.

For a minority of Korean Chinese with whom I speak, acquiring South Korean citizenship is the most decisive way to align their emotional, cultural, and historical claims with their legal identities as Koreans. For example, Hee Sook says, "If someone asked me to choose between Chinese and South Korean citizenship, I think I would probably choose South Korean now. It's not that I hate China. But after living eight years here, I have come to learn things that I didn't know before." Although Hee Sook attended Korean Chinese schools through high school, she says she realized that "in China, we learned very little about Joseon history. There are three sentences about Joseon history." Moving to Seoul has given her the opportunity to learn more about South Korea specifically, and "[her own] history as a Korean." Though Hee Sook does not state any desired specific political or economic outcomes, Koreanness has value to her, and South Korean citizenship would be a meaningful and tangible acknowledgement of her historical ties to South Korea. Hee Sook and Sung Bae are exceptions among the Korean Chinese in the study. Rather than arguing for outright citizenship, a more common strategy to secure better treatment in South Korea is to argue, as Kyeong Won in the opening anecdote does, that Korean Chinese—by virtue of their ties to Joseon, the last incarnation of a united Korean homeland—are the "original" Koreans and deserve more respect.

Determining ethnic authenticity and who is "really" Korean based on cultural arguments does not seem to follow logical rules. For example, if we were to use language proficiency as the standard for judging who is more "Korean," then most Korean Americans would fall short. An example of my own linguistic shortcomings happened when asking a discussion question to the students in my English class at the Korean Chinese church. I inadvertently used the Korean counting word[6] for animals (*mari*) rather than for people (*myeong*), an error that only a very young child or a beginner's-level Korean language learner would make. Everyone started laughing immediately, and Song Lim even clawed at the air while meowing loudly. This blunder became a recurring joke throughout the year. Korean Chinese from my class would ask me questions about myself beginning with "how many," such as "How many siblings do you have?" or "How many children do you want?" using the animal counting word—insinuating that I came from a family of animals. My protestations about the confusing rules of Korean language fell on unsympathetic ears as my students pointed out that English grammar and spelling had countless "exceptions," which, I conceded, was a valid point.

There were many such moments of humor around my frequent mistakes in Korean, but they also shed light on a more serious issue. Most Korean Chinese in the study, even into the third generation, are fluent or highly proficient speakers, while most Korean Americans rate their Korean language skills at the high-beginner or low-intermediate level. My Korean Chinese students do not tease me for my deficient language skills as a personal critique but to point out the inconsistent reception of return migrants by South Koreans. It stands to reason that if South Korean national identity is still defined by the notion of shared ancestry and culture, then South Korea should not exclude a community of people who actually embody these characteristics.

Many Korean Chinese use *cultural* arguments about ethnic authenticity to undercut the legitimacy of South Korea as the gatekeeper to ethnic inclusion. In diaspora and transnational studies, the notion of authenticity is often assumed to rest in the "homeland" as the geographical space from which the diaspora originates. However, with a divided homeland into two nations still at war, the question of whether "authenticity" is rooted in North or South Korea is already in dispute. Korean Chinese use language to justify why they should be seen as the possessors of "authentic" culture, not South Koreans. Kyeong Mi, a third-generation Korean Chinese woman, explains, "Our mother language is *joseon mal*, not *hanguk mal*." ("Mal" translates in English to "language.") The former is framed as an uncorrupted language true to the original characters put in place when Korean was created, while the latter has been modified over time through modernization of vocabulary and increased hybridization with English.

The idea of cultural "authenticity" when applied to language is complicated because of language's dynamic, rather than fixed, nature. Originally, nearly 75 percent of Korean vocabulary had Chinese roots (*hanja*), but many hanja-based words have been deliberately replaced with Korean characters or English words. In line with this change, South Korean schools have gradually reduced instruction on the thousands of Chinese characters in the past few decades. As a result, many younger South Koreans have a limited knowledge of hanja characters compared to older generations. Korean Chinese critique contemporary South Koreans for this loss of knowledge of the "original" Chinese characters. Hye Soon, the Korean Chinese domestic worker introduced in chapter 2, resents that South Koreans treat Korean Chinese like "people who are lower than them in all aspects." While many Korean Chinese, especially labor migrants, do not have college degrees, Hye Soon notes, "there are a lot of South Koreans my age who don't know the alphabet. . . . There are some people who don't know their own names! . . . But South Koreans think that we are uneducated or unschooled, or how should I say this, are kind of dumb."[7] Many Korean Chinese are well aware of the fact that South Koreans dismiss joseon mal as outdated, or as *saturi* (local dialects often associated with "country" people who are less educated and less sophisticated than urban residents from Seoul). Even though all languages, not just Korean, change over time, the preservation of tradition is important to Korean Chinese like Hye Soon. The problem is that joseon mal and the cultural capital of Korean Chinese have little status or importance in contemporary South Korea. Comparing their situation to Korean Americans, Korean Chinese find it illogical that they are dismissed as uneducated, unsophisticated, outdated, or even not Korean at all, while Korean Americans, despite their linguistic and cultural deficiencies, are treated better.

The favored status of Korean Americans is not the only example of inconsistent rules of national membership within the diaspora. North Korean political migrants in South Korea who are granted access to South Korean citizenship provide more evidence for Korean Chinese of unfair ethnic exclusion practices. While Korean Chinese push for better treatment in South Korea because they have *more* Korean cultural capital than Korean Americans, they also argue that they are *culturally* similar to North Koreans by virtue of their shared bloodlines and ancestry. As such, Korean Chinese should also be eligible to the generous economic, political, and social aid given to North Koreans by the South Korean state.

The Impact of North–South Korean Politics on Korean Chinese

The dissolution of Joseon into two separate and warring nations after 1945 complicates issues of identity and national belonging in both North and South Korea as well as for the Korean diaspora.[8] The geographic proximity of North Korea to China means that Korean Chinese in Yanbian Prefecture often have had consistent interactions with North Koreans and nearly no contact with South Koreans prior to their return migration trips. Cities in Yanbian Prefecture and surrounding provinces are often the first stop in a long and dangerous journey for North Koreans escaping across the Tumen River. As a result, many Korean Chinese living in these areas feel a strong sense of obligation to help them by offering food, money, and even shelter from authorities.[9] Most Korean Chinese I speak with trace their ancestral hometowns to present-day North Korea. Many traveled there to see family and were, in turn, visited by their North Korean relatives throughout their childhoods.

"*Talbukja* can get citizenship, but Korean Chinese cannot. I guess it makes sense that North Koreans would feel more strongly connected to South Korea because they were the same country not that long ago. That connection is not as strong for Korean Chinese."[10] This is how Soon Hee, a twenty-seven-year old third-generation Korean Chinese graduate student, describes the differences between the relationship of North Koreans and Korean Chinese to South Koreans. While she has found her experiences in South Korea over the past year to be mostly positive, Soon Hee is keenly aware of the hardships that many Korean Chinese face. Unlike educational migrants, she knows that labor migrants often struggle with the burdens of undocumented status. She points out, "South Koreans treat North Koreans better. They give them apartments, and they help them. South Koreans don't treat Korean Chinese well because they just see them as here to work. North Koreans live better here in South Korea than Korean Chinese."

Anthropologist Byung-Ho Chung notes the range of terms used to refer to North Koreans in South Korea such as "political defectors," "refugee migrants," members of the "ethnic-Korean diaspora," or "cultural minorities."[11] Importantly, all these different categories stress the *political* nature of these migrations as well as the shared *familial* ties between South and North Koreans. Korean Chinese argue that while this criterion applies to them as well, they are largely classified as *economic* and *foreign* migrants, ignoring the historical and political contexts that prevented their return from China. Passed in 1997, the Act on the Protection and Resettlement Support for the Residents Who Escaped from North Korea guarantees economic aid from the South Korean state as well as other services such as job training and housing subsidies, and educational, psychological, and cultural services as part of their resettlement process.[12]

Many Korean Chinese resent their ineligibility for these same benefits, a situation made worse because they are often treated as criminals. As Kwang Soo puts it, "historically . . . North Koreans and Korean Chinese share the same blood. But in South Korea, Korean Chinese have to live by avoiding the police, James Bond–style, while . . . the government gives citizenship to North Koreans . . . and housing, food, [and] clothing is provided and taken care of." He concludes, "The laws enforced by the South Korean government toward Korean Chinese and North Koreans are unfair, but regretfully, no one complains." From the perspective of Korean Chinese, they are once again excluded, while

North Koreans and Korean Americans receive preferential treatment under South Korean immigration laws based on their shared Korean ancestry.

Reversing these policies would not be a simple process. A proposal offering South Korean citizenship and resettlement aid for Korean Chinese return migrants would create political tensions with China, particularly if it triggered a large-scale exodus of Chinese citizens to South Korea. In fact, most Korean Chinese in the study have no intention of becoming South Korean citizens. Their references to North Koreans are largely about equal recognition of family ties for all communities within the Korean diaspora. As citizens who have benefited from policies toward national minorities that allow them to retain their cultural and ethnic identities, Korean Chinese would also face many difficulties repatriating to a newly unified peninsula. Kyeong Won asks, "If North Korea and South Korea do reunify, will they take Korean Chinese back? . . . China would not let all Korean Chinese just disappear." She believes ethnic identities are ultimately secondary to the obligations of Korean Chinese to the Chinese state as citizens. In addition, there is little evidence that South Koreans would welcome future Korean Chinese arriving en masse given their current treatment of those already in residence.

Chung notes a great deal of "ambiguity and arbitrariness found in defining legal and cultural membership in South Korea," which, in turn, creates and sustains the hierarchies between return migrant communities such as North Koreans and Korean Chinese.[13] Much of this vagueness around ethnic membership is shaped by the current political climate on the Korean peninsula. The South Korean state gains political goodwill in the eyes of the international community by welcoming migrants willing to brave a treacherous journey to escape the "oppressive" North Korean regime and find "safety" and freedom in the South. In so doing, South Korea supports its claims over North Korea as the sole sovereign power on the peninsula. Rather than cultural difference or shared blood and ancestry, political histories between North and South Korea become the basis for ethnic inclusion for

North Koreans in South Korea and ethnic exclusion for Korean Chinese migrants who offer little, if any, political benefit to the South Korean state.

Like many Korean Chinese I speak with, Kwang Soo believes in the possibility of reunification, or *tongil*:

> The possible key to reunification may even be Korean Chinese. . . . The division between the North and South has been well over fifty years. The only people who can break down this barrier are Korean Chinese. Can the Japanese, Chinese, or Americans do such a job? I don't think so. . . . Joseon was separated for thirty-six humiliating years under Japanese control, during which time Korean Chinese crossed over to China. I don't know when it will be, but when the time for reunification comes, I firmly believe that there will be work for us Korean Chinese to do.

Interestingly, any discussion of reunification is largely absent from my conversations with Korean Americans, except for two who have an active interest in South Korean politics. For Korean Chinese, a (re)unified peninsula would signify a return to Joseon and a single nation, which would recognize all return migrant communities equally. With their established ties with both North and South Korea, Korean Chinese, unlike Korean Americans, could play valuable roles as ambassadors. Kwang Soo notes that in the past, brokered visits reuniting family members separated because of the Korean War have taken place in China, already marking it as a "neutral" space in the political crisis between North and South Korea. However, recent aggressive acts taken by the North Korean state, including the testing of ballistic missiles and nuclear weaponry, and the continued presence of United States and South Korean military forces in the demilitarized zone (DMZ) make reunification, at least in the near future, an extremely unlikely prospect.

"Korean Chinese are suffering in South Korea without citizenship." With this statement, Hye Soon acknowledges that the core of the economic and social struggles of Korean Chinese in South Korea is their Chinese citizenship. The returns of ethnic migrants like North Koreans, Korean Americans, and Korean Chinese highlight the gap between an *ethnic identity* based on shared ancestry and histories and a *national identity* rooted in citizenship to a nation-state in the South Korean context.

Counteridentities within Korean Chinese "Geo-ethnic Bubbles"

"People always ask, 'Are you Korean or Chinese?'" Even though Chul Mu has lived in South Korea for over ten years, at times as an undocumented laborer and now as the legal spouse of a South Korean citizen, he is still asked this question regularly by South Koreans. Chul Mu feels there is no easy answer because "in China, Korean Chinese are seen as Korean, but in South Korea, Korean Chinese are seen as Chinese." Perhaps because Korean Chinese are seen as neither "really" Korean nor Chinese in whatever national context they find themselves, Korean Chineseness is built on a fusion of Korean and Chinese cultural attributes and their historical ties to the Korean peninsula. But because of experiences with social and economic discrimination in South Korea, Korean Chineseness takes on a more political purpose. According to anthropologist Takeyuki Tsuda, "ethnic counteridentities arise when minority groups maintain a sense of ethnic difference in opposition to majority society."[14] Rather than feeling more strongly "Korean" from their physical returns to their ancestral homeland, Korean Chinese take pride in the ways they differ from South Koreans. Korean Chineseness is nurtured within spaces that I call "geo-ethnic bubbles," which are geographically bound, symbolically demarcated, socially insular, and culturally distinct.

The bubbles of Korean Americans and Korean Chinese have little to no overlap and are similarly insular. It is telling that for almost all Korean Chinese in the study, I am the only Korean American with whom they have direct contact. Similarly, Korean American respondents have little to no regular exposure to Korean Chinese. In fact, most are unaware of the large number of Korean Chinese in South Korea or the struggles they face. "Outsiders" can transgress into other bubbles of hybridity, as was the case of Song Lim at TGI Fridays in Hongdae at the beginning of the book or myself at the Korean Chinese church, but it is through invitation by an "insider."

Like in most major metropolitan cities, communities of similar backgrounds concentrate within small, scattered neighborhoods in Seoul as a result of residential segregation by class, race, and/or ethnicity.[15] Tangible evidence of hybridity is visible in geographically concentrated Korean Chinese spaces. For example, the immediate neighborhood surrounding the church in Yeongdeungpo-gu caters heavily to the Korean Chinese community, as evidenced by posted signs and advertisements containing a mix of Chinese and Korean characters. Cheap calling cards to China are displayed in shop windows nearby, and most shops and restaurants are staffed by Korean Chinese. On the grounds of the church itself, community members seamlessly switch between Korean and Chinese in the same conversation.[16] Migrants use the church as a safe site to network and find fellowship with other Korean Chinese.

For the most part, Korean Chinese in the study generally have tight social networks with other Korean Chinese. For example, many educational migrants participate in a graduate student organization that connects them to other Korean Chinese rather than international students more broadly within the local academic community. Korean Chinese occasionally socialize with some Chinese or South Koreans, but no one had friends who were Korean Americans or other members of the Korean diaspora. "Comfort" and cultural commonalities are often used to account for their tendencies to socialize with mostly other Korean Chinese. As Kyeong Won explains, "When I meet South Koreans . . . there is a cultural difference. . . . If I am with Korean Chinese, I can talk comfortably. With South Koreans, that doesn't happen. It is stressful and uncomfortable." These Korean Chinese social circles subtly reinforce the line between themselves and South Koreans as well as between themselves and other return migrant communities.

Some of the transnational practices of Korean Chinese are localized to Seoul itself and would not be performed if they were back in China. One Korean Chinese reinvention of an "authentic" ethnic tradition is their engagement with chuseok. Chuseok, one of the most important Korean holidays of the year, is a time of reflection when most South Koreans return to their hometown villages to pay their respects to their ancestors and honor the good harvest with a feast of traditional offerings. During this period, the normally chaotic streets of Seoul become uncharacteristically quiet as many South Koreans leave the capital for the countryside. Yet in a large open area near Seoul's Han River, a vibrant chuseok celebration takes place, weaving together new and traditional Korean customs, that befits a transnational community straddling roots in both China and South Korea.

I overhear snippets of conversation in both Chinese and Korean as I stand with a large crowd of people watching the singers and dancers on the central stage dressed in *hanbok*, traditional Korean dresses of bright greens, blues, pinks, and yellows. Occasionally, when the emcee calls out the names of different cities in Yanbian Province, crowd members cheer in response to their hometowns. I run into Yu Na and Hye Soon, the two women who invited me to the celebration. They greet me enthusiastically and press a box of round, thick Chinese moon cakes into my hands before disappearing into the crowd of people to dispense more of the pastries.

Although to a casual passerby, the festival would not seem unusual, the very fact that it is a public celebration of an occasion that is usually a private family affair can be interpreted in two different ways. On one hand, it can serve as a reminder of how fundamentally out of place Korean Chinese are in their ancestral homeland. But in South Korea, away from their hometowns and families, this gathering of Korean Chinese is also an acknowledgment of their shared predicament. They are unable to return to the families they left behind while simultaneously unable to fulfill their duties in ancestral hometowns in South Korea. The call-and-response between the emcee and crowd, using cities in Yanbian, amends traditional practices that reflect their identities as simultaneously Korean and not Korean. Linguistic switching between Korean and Chinese alongside the enjoyment of traditional Chinese pastries highlights the strong presence of their Chinese identities on one of the most "Korean" holidays of the year.

On the other hand, this gathering can also be read as a positive affirmation of Korean Chineseness through communal ritual. In contrast to the dominant narrative in South Korea about Korean Chinese—undocumented, uneducated, unskilled, dirty, poor people to be pitied, or evading the police "James Bond–style"—these Korean Chinese are highly visible and festive. Reverend Seo serves as the main pastor at the Korean Chinese church where I conducted my fieldwork and is one of the leaders of the NGO that is based there. He takes the microphone during a break between performances. After his introductory remarks, Reverend Seo's tone becomes more serious as he praises the community for their bravery and strength despite all the challenges they have faced in South Korea. As staff members circulate collection jars through the crowd, a photo of a young boy in his late teens is projected on the screen on the stage. Reverend Seo tells the story of the young boy, his serious health conditions, and the high cost of treatment that he can only receive in South Korea. He then speaks about the obligation Korean Chinese have to help those in their community struggling to survive. The money collected that day would help ease the financial burdens on the young boy's mother, Eun Mi, who came to Seoul to take care of her son, leaving her husband and daughter behind. Eun Mi balances her duties as a domestic worker with frequent trips to the hospital with her son for treatments. As members of the Korean Chinese community, Reverend Seo urges those in attendance to give as much as they can because, like them, Eun Mi and her son came to South Korea for a better life and deserve the opportunity to realize their dreams.

Conclusion

In the context of "diasporic returns" of Japanese Americans to Japan, sociologist Jane Yamashiro observes "the notion of diaspora assumes that the homeland is the ethnic center and causes forms of ethnic culture outside of the ancestral homeland to be seen as less authentic."[17] Yamashiro questions these conventions about diaspora–homeland relations, noting that while "Japan is typically viewed as the place from which Japanese culture originates, it is not the contemporary center of Japanese culture for all people of Japanese ancestry."[18] Because hybridized cultural forms emerge over generations in diasporic communities outside of the homeland, meanings of ethnicity can be varied, distinct, and locally authentic. In this chapter, I have shown how Korean Chinese use their ethnic counteridentities to push back on South Korea's claim as the cultural and political center of Koreanness. Built on the historical logic of ethnic authenticity, Korean Chinese contest the South Korean nationalist project by *co-opting* the same discourse around the close relationship of ethnicity and nationalism used by South Koreans to exclude them. In so doing, Korean Chinese respondents find a narrative that legitimates their place in South Korea as Koreans despite their systematic exclusion from the F-4 visa available to Korean Americans, as well as the citizenship and state aid granted to North Korean political migrants.

The counteridentities of Korean Chinese in the study are substantively different from Korean Americans. "Exiled" in China because of the division of the Korean peninsula, many grew up in Yanbian Prefecture, where they attended schools in which instruction was in Korean and Chinese and lived in towns where signs were routinely in Korean and Chinese. Unlike Korean Americans, who benefit economically and socially from the privileged position of the United States and the West more broadly in South Korea, Korean Chinese must use their counteridentities as a mobilizing strategy to advocate for equal treatment by South Koreans as members of the diaspora. "Geo-ethnic bubbles" built from insulated social networks and segregated neighborhoods are important spaces that bring Korean Chinese closer together in Seoul as a community. This can be the foundation for celebration, as is evidenced in the chuseok celebration, but also a source of economic and social support for Korean Chinese in need like Eun Mi and her son.

5

The Logics of Cosmopolitan
Koreanness and Global Citizenship

Shil mang (disappointment), Everything is so *shilmangseoro* (disappointing). I can't believe my parents came from this filth. I was living in Sinchon, you know. There is garbage everywhere and throw-up everywhere. People are clueless, they act so stupid. . . . I felt so embarrassed. . . . It is a huge disappointment . . . Wow, this is a different civilization and it's nothing to be proud of. And shit, my family is from here, I still have family here, and it's so embarrassing. . . . Growing up, my parents always said, 'Korea is like this, Koreans are like this. Koreans are very generous, kind and considerate, Koreans are yielding, very educated, [have] good manners. Koreans are the best. . . .' It's something that my father always said, and so I always had this idea that [South] Korea is great. I mean, when you come to visit, [South] Korea is great. . . . When you live here, you see all the dirt and grime that's beneath it. I wasn't prepared for it.

Maya says this to me as we sit on the balcony of her apartment, sharing a bowl of juicy dark-purple grapes. It is clear that the South Korea she has been living in for the past two years has not lived up to the expectations she held of South Korea and Koreanness prior

to her arrival. Before moving to South Korea, Maya had a successful career in the IT industry. But, she says, "after the last project, I
thought, 'This sucks.' So I went backpacking. It ended up being five
months. . . . I came to [South] Korea because I [didn't] have any
money and I [didn't] want to go home." In addition to working
and saving money, Maya hoped the move to Seoul would improve
her Korean language skills and allow her to become closer with her
relatives, with whom she had had little substantive contact while
growing up in California. However, over the last two years, she
has fulfilled neither of these goals. Instead, her disappointment in
contemporary South Korea and her negative impressions of South
Korean culture has led her to question her once strong sense of
pride in her ethnic identity.

In this chapter, I show how the physical return to the ancestral homeland is a pivotal experience for Korean Americans and
Korean Chinese in the study. Many stop identifying as hyphenated
outsiders who belong "neither here nor there" and embrace identities as true transnational actors who possess the mental flexibility
and adaptability to survive and thrive wherever they go. They do
so by asserting "cosmopolitan Koreanness" as a strategy to position
themselves as better global citizens in relation to South Koreans.
In addition, this cosmopolitanism gives them valuable economic
and social advantages over the dominant group back in their home
countries—namely, White Americans in the United States and
ethnic Han in China.

Crisis into Opportunity: Cosmopolitan "Dispositions" and "Competencies"

Social scientists have explored the difficulties of the "mobility of
the hyphen," particularly when adult returnees migrate to an ancestral homeland only to feel more foreign than part of the family
because of the linguistic and culture challenges they face.[1] The difficulties of living and working with homeland ethnics reveal the
multiple ways of creating and performing "authentic" ethnicity. For
example, in her work on adult second-generation Greek Canadian

and Greek Australian "returnees," Georgina Tsolidis notes many found fault with Greece as too dirty and Greek society as too traditional. As a result, most felt more alienated from their previously strong Greek heritage. Similarly, in the opening narrative, Maya focuses on the "filth," "garbage," and "throw-up" on the streets that make her embarrassed for South Korea and angry at South Koreans who critique her for not being "Korean" enough. The problem is that many Korean Chinese and Korean Americans "return" to South Korea to escape the discrimination and racism they face in their home countries, but are unprepared to face new forms of discrimination and feelings of marginalization in a "homeland" that is decidedly not the same Korea their parents or grandparents left behind. But Min Ji, a thirty-year-old Korean American woman, focuses on the advantages of the immigrant condition that allow for a different, more constructive narrative to emerge:

> I guess . . . I've "returned," a subconscious return to Korea, a return to Seoul National [University] Hospital where I was born. . . . There are times when it's really good, and sometimes it's absurd. What I'm feeling and you're feeling, that confusion and overwhelming feeling, is experienced by our parents [as] immigrants in America. . . . That feeling can be experienced by anyone who has made a choice to change or [were] forced to make a change in a physical sense. My mother always tells me, "You are so lucky . . . because you can live anywhere you want."

With these words, Min Ji connects her own decision to move back to Seoul to that of her parents' immigration history many decades earlier. Min Ji was born in Seoul and immigrated with her family to the United States at the age of four. She grew up in a predominantly White upper-middle-class suburb of Philadelphia, but feels like her "parents ensured that [her] Koreanness [was] fully realized" by teaching her and her brother Korean language, literature, and history while growing up. Min Ji cites a Korean saying based on four Chinese characters, known as *sajaseongeo*, to explain the idea of finding strength in the challenges of the immigrant condition: "*Chun hwa wei bok*. It refers to a situation that looked bad [but] has turned around to be very good. . . . In Chinese, the character for 'crisis'—it's 'crisis' and 'opportunity' in the same one. Within something as hopeless as a crisis, there is opportunity. That's the same with identity crisis. . . . That's what I think. In this globalized whatever, you have an added perspective."

What Min Ji calls "an added perspective" in this "globalized whatever," is another way of talking about what some researchers label "cosmopolitanism." Ulf Hannerz defines cosmopolitanism as "an intellectual and aesthetic stance of openness toward divergent cultural experiences, a search for contrasts rather than uniformity."[2] Cosmopolitanism is also "a matter of competence" that enables an individual to "make one's way into other cultures, through listening, looking, intuiting and reflecting."[3] This competence allows people who possess it the advantage of "manoeuvring more or less expertly with a particular system of meanings and meaningful forms."[4] Building on this definition, Hiroki Igarashi and Hiro Saito argue cosmopolitanism represents an "*embodied state* of cultural capital" which includes "both *dispositions* of openness to foreign others and cultures and *competencies* to enact such openness with ease."[5] Rather than devalued as people who belong nowhere, Min Ji and other return migrants in the study see the merits of being transnational actors who have ties to more than one nation simultaneously. Raised in immigrant families whose lives have been built on mobility and exposed to different kinds of cultures from an early age, Korean Americans and Korean Chinese in the study recognize they possess a wide range of tools in their "cultural toolkit" and are creative in their usage depending on their context

Claiming "cosmopolitan Koreanness" accomplishes two goals for return migrants. One is to define the characteristics of cosmopolitan Koreanness embodied by Korean Americans and Korean Chinese that make them distinct from and "better" than South Koreanness. The second is how this capital empowers return migrants to see themselves as global citizens with better economic and cultural futures than the dominant reference group back in the United States and China. On both levels, cosmopolitan Koreanness gives them the language to resist the marginalization they experience in the ancestral "homeland" as well as their "home" countries of citizenship. However, the advantages of global citizenship are uneven because the global cultural capital of Korean Americans is routinely accorded more value than that of Korean Chinese. Using South Korea as a case study, I show that, ultimately, global citizenship is a framework that maintains and reproduces hierarchies that reflect the position of nation-states in the global economy.

Better Global Citizens than South Koreans

Bourdieu and other scholars of culture have argued that cultural capital, working in tandem with other forms of capital like human and economic, creates status hierarchies. Cultural arguments give return migrants the moral high ground from which they can critique South Koreans, and cosmopolitanism is an example of this. The influx of new ideas, technology, cultures, and people as a result of dramatic economic and political transformations in South Korea does not necessarily mean the ideologies of South Koreans have kept pace. In fact, both Korean Americans and Korean Chinese in the study find fault with South Koreans for lacking the dispositions and competencies that exemplify a more "global" mind-set.

One common critique is with South Korea's hypermaterialism and the conscious display of brand-name, luxury goods to signal one's social class. Myeong Dae is a thirty-two-year-old single third-generation Korean Chinese man who has lived in South Korea for the past three years. He has moved from employer to employer on short-term contracts, a process that has become more difficult because of tighter immigration policies for foreign migrant workers and fewer available jobs. Myeong Dae speaks to the negative influence of capitalism and consumerism in South Korean society around him in this way, "If you look at [South Korea's] culture today, you see people drinking and clubbing and [going to] karaoke. . . . Women especially learn to easily like things like makeup and clothes. A lot of people fall into this culture. . . . The world focuses so much on material things like clothes and makeup, so it's impossible not to fall into such things."

Given the many sacrifices Myeong Dae has made to live in South Korea to work in 3-D (difficult, dirty, and dangerous) industries, it is perhaps unsurprising that he sees South Koreans as mindless consumers and materialistic. A precarious visa status and the stigma of being an undereducated, unskilled laborer contribute to his choice to live an ascetic lifestyle in which "drinking and clubbing and karaoke" are largely absent. Myeong Dae's disdain for the consumerism and materialism of South Korea is one shared by many Korean Chinese respondents. Korean Chinese labor migrants speak often about delayed gratification, enduring emotional and economic hardships in Seoul for a better future. They take pride in making do with less in the present so that they can send larger remittances that make tangible differences back home in China, such as better housing, home improvements, and greater educational opportunities. While most South Koreans "see [Korean Chinese] as low-wage workers doing dirty jobs," Kyeong Won points out, "if you look at the situation, actually Korean Chinese are better off than South Koreans here. . . . Our parents live in nice apartments in China. What are they talking about?" She locates the cultural attributes of Korean Chineseness in hard work, sacrifice, and filial duty, while defining South Koreanness by excess consumption and mindlessness.

While Myeong Dae concedes that hyperconsumerism is not a failing exclusive to South Koreans, Chun Ja, a Korean American woman, is more unsparing in her critiques. She tells me she feels like a "fake Korean," and this is a good thing because "real" South Koreans, especially women from the middle and upper-middle class, are "obsessed" with brands. As she explains,

There's something that rubs me the wrong way about the way Koreans like to flaunt wealth even when they don't have it.

There's something nouveau riche about it all. . . . It's about being poor. When you don't have much, you fantasize about supposedly the best things in life. Consumerism is a relatively new concept in a developing country like Korea. In the US, there's an anti-consumerist attitude in youth. Most of my friends make their clothes; consumerism is treated cautiously by young people in the US. In Korea, it's rampant and guilt-free. There's no PC-ness of trying to correct it. Explosion[s] of brands, people who want really expensive things that they can't afford and go into debt. . . . There's something about wealth, looking like you have a lot of money, that Koreans are really into.

Despite their dissimilar social and economic positions in South Korea and their upbringings in different national contexts—one communist, one capitalist—Chun Ja and Myeong Dae are both critical of South Korea's excess. In both cases, this critique enables them to see their own group's more tempered relationship to consumerism, a reflection of the dispositions and competencies linked to cosmopolitanism. However, the argument that Chun Ja makes—that many of her friends in the United States are more thoughtful consumers—says more about her youth, political ideology, and socioeconomic class than about Americans more broadly. A cursory look at US media, including reality shows centered on wealthy celebrities such as the highly successful "House-wives" franchise and print advertising, confirms that Americans value brands like Gucci, Louis Vuitton, and other high-priced goods as well as beauty products and plastic surgery as markers of high status.

But categorizing South Koreans as uncritical "nouveau riche" aligns with Korean Americans' assumptions about South Korea as a fundamentally poor, developing nation. For example, Jessica confesses that she expected South Korea "[was] going to be a lot more third world" despite knowing that it is "the eleventh-largest financial power in the world." Pigeon-holing Koreans as culturally deficient enables a lack of self-critique regarding the ways Americans engage in the same kinds of behaviors themselves. Chun Ja readily admits that in Seoul, the social activities that she and her group of friends engage in largely revolve around "drinking, singing, or drinking and singing at the same time." However, when it comes to overspending and consumption of luxury goods, they as Americans are less likely to fall into this trap because it isn't a new phenomenon. The United States has a highly industrialized economy and has historically been one of the leading nations economically in the Western world. In contrast, South Korea's rapid transformation from a "third world" to newly industrialized country and the growth of a middle class with disposable income has occurred during their lifetimes. As a result, Korean Americans are different from and better than South Koreans, whose cultural mind-sets as citizens of a "developing" nation have not caught up with the rapid economic and political changes in the last few decades.

In addition to hyperconsumerism, other critiques from Korean Chinese and Korean American respondents are rooted in mobility and open-mindedness—two dispositional characteristics of cosmopolitan Koreanness. For example, Soo Young's recounting of a funny interaction with a South Korean customer serves as an example of Korean Chinese critiques of the parochial *sagobangshik*, or "mind-set," of contemporary South Koreans. Soo Young is a second-generation Korean Chinese woman in her midthirties, who grew up in Yanbian Prefecture in a town with a large, stable population of Korean Chinese. Her dry sense of humor initially made it difficult for me to tell whether she was serious or joking. When she worked at a nursery, Soo Young said a South Korean *ajuma* (a middle-aged woman) held up a strawberry close to her face and asked if she had ever seen one before. When I dismiss this as another joke, Soo Young insists that this really happened. The woman's question was not motivated out of a genuine curiosity about Soo Young's life back in China, but reflected that "kind of feeling that [South Koreans] are looking down on us." While unspoken, Soo Young also felt that the South Korean woman assumed that her economic circumstances in China were so low that she would not have been able to afford something so exotic as a strawberry. She shares another instance of South Korean ignorance: "When I first came to South Korea, someone asked me what China was like, what do they have there. As a joke, I said there is no moon and there are no stars. She totally believed me."

Soo Young uses these two experiences to critique South Koreans who assume that people from "poorer" nations lack the same range of experiences as themselves and the repeated dismissals of Korean Chinese cultural capital as obsolete and "too traditional" by South Korean standards. She is angered that many of these South Koreans see China, especially Yanbian, as a place so foreign to them that South Korea and Yanbian could not possibly have anything in common, including the same moon, sun, and stars. Moreover, South Koreans hold steadfast in the belief that Chinese cities are undeveloped and that Korean Chinese live in a world without exposure to luxury goods, like strawberries, that are commonplace in Seoul. Soo Young uses the inability of the South Koreans in the two stories above to imagine what it is like in another country as a lack of competence. In contrast, many Korean Chinese point to their histories as migrants who have uprooted their lives to start new ones in South Korea as proof that their mind-sets are broader and more flexible. As Chung Ae explains, "South Korea might be advanced, but South Korean people don't seem to know much. We may live in China, but we are aware of what's going on in the world, advances in the world." From her perspective, "people who have traveled around a lot, they are better." This last statement is in response to her experiences with South Korean coworkers and employers who routinely talk down to her as one of the few foreigners employed in the research center but who themselves have few experiences living or traveling abroad.

Korean Chinese also use the value of open-mindedness and comfort with diversity to elevate their status with respect to South Koreans. They do so by referring often to China's multicultural policies that protect and promote autonomy for officially recognized national minority groups. Their adaptability as a national minority means that they can shift fluidly from majority ethnic Han spaces at work or school to Korean-dominated spaces at home with little effort. They have been indoctrinated with the belief that in China, national minorities like ethnic Koreans only increase China's strength as a unified yet diverse nation.

Korean Americans offer similar arguments that South Koreans lack the necessary skills in a globalizing world to engage competently with diversity and multiculturalism. Sae Il puts it this way: "South Koreans have an unbelievably narrow construction of Korean identity. Shop in the same department store, same news, same clothes, same consumption patterns, same educational systems, shared military experience for men. South Koreans are homogenous. . . . The 'monoculture' in Seoul [is] an outcome of South Korea's racial demographics and myth of ethnic homogeneity that manifests in the inflexibility of people's attitudes and actions." Interestingly, this position actually does not align with the experiences with racism and discrimination that Sae Il and many other Korean Americans have faced growing up in the United States. While they may be critical of multiculturalism while in the United States, in South Korea, their "American point of view" makes Korean Americans different from and better than South Koreans because they are able to express their individuality in the face of the pressure to conform.

The negative characterizations of South Koreans as monocultural and closed-minded allow both Korean Americans and Korean Chinese to see themselves as better "global citizens" because they have grown up in diverse national contexts in which Koreanness is an asset. Their exclusion as not "really" Korean in South Korea due to cultural deficits becomes an opportunity to attack South Koreans for gatekeeping a very narrow and insular meaning of Koreanness that is increasingly outdated in a globalizing world.

Korean Americans and Korean Chinese in the study also critique South Korea's perceived willingness to sacrifice "authentic" Korean culture in the blind pursuit of Westernization. Before coming to South Korea, many Korean Americans expressed desires to immerse themselves in Korean traditions and culture, improving their language skills and learning more about the history of their ancestral homeland. But instead, they are confronted by streets peppered with Dunkin' Donuts, Starbucks, McDonalds, and Pizza Hut on every corner. In effect, Seoul looks like any major US city, like Manhattan or Los Angeles–a disappointing reality for Korean Americans who come in search of a "real" Korea. Sang Hee is a 1.5-generation woman who did not immigrate to the United States until she was seventeen. Unlike most Korean Americans in the study, she has significant memories from her childhood in South Korea and has had sustained regular contact with South Korea throughout her life. Over her last few visits, Sang Hee has seen an acceleration of the visible presence of Westernization to the point where now "it's very Korean to be Western." She does not see this attitude as aberrant but instead as commonly held by many upwardly mobile South Koreans.

Ironically, Korean Americans benefit economically from this desire by South Koreans to acquire Western cultural capital; their livelihoods contribute to this erosion of the "authentic" Korean culture. From the perspective of Korean Americans as people who have grown up in the United States, it is only natural that they are fluent in English and immersed in American culture. However, when South Koreans aspire to improve their English proficiency and consume Western products, Korean Americans interpret these behaviors as signs of weakness rather than cosmopolitanism. This speaks to the ways Korean Americans *need* South Korea to be more "traditional" because that is what they see as "Korean." South Korea and Korean culture is expected to remain fixed in time to the era of their parents' memories from the 1960s and 1970s.

Looking for a more "authentic" Korea, some Korean Americans leave the congested hustle-bustle of Seoul for places that are "more sincere." For example, Sae Il says his mixed-race identity makes it nearly impossible for South Koreans to see him as legitimately South Korean. But "When I go to the *sigol*"—countryside—"I receive much less discrimination, less attacks on my identity. People in Seoul struggle with issues of legitimacy more than those outside of Seoul." Sae Il romanticizes the countryside as where "authentic" South Korea exists because there are less visible impacts of Westernization. Maya experienced a similar feeling of relief when she left Seoul and moved to Jeju, a tropical island off the southern coast often described as "the Korean version of Hawai'i." There, Maya encountered people who she saw as "more basic, they don't seem to be always chasing after the money." She continues, "They don't seem to want to get to know me just because I [speak] English . . . probably like the [South] Korea that my parents left."

These expectations reflect a lack of awareness of the transformations that South Korea has undergone in the decades since their parents emigrated. Rather than seeing culture as fluid and dynamic, Korean Americans interpret these changes within a fixed binary in which the United States and South Korea represent "modernity" and "tradition" with no room for overlap. As a result, Korean Americans see the cost of Westernization in contemporary South Korea as an erasure of what is uniquely Korean. Maya concludes that South Koreans are in "this void, they have no culture. . . . They have got these blinders on, all they're looking for is the money." The critique of Korean Americans by South Koreans for their lack of Korean cultural capital as "too American" is redirected back at South Korea for having no culture at all.

Many Korean Chinese also are critical of what they perceive as a deliberate loss of Korea's rich cultural traditions and centuries of history in the face of Westernization. But their starting positions differ from Korean Americans in that the "Korea" their parents and grandparents left is rooted in an even older "original" Koreanness as discussed in the previous chapter. From the perspective of Korean Chinese, not only are South Koreans deficient in their knowledge of Chinese characters (hanja) at the root of the original Korean language, but Korean Chinese are also critical of the way English has become part of the South Korean lexicon. For Korean Chinese graduate students, this shift creates additional challenges. Dong Moon notes that in many classes, his professors assign readings in English and use English terminology often in their lectures. Korean Chinese international students are at a disadvantage as compared to their South Korean peers, many of whom have had English classes as part of their curriculum from an early age and attended additional language classes at private learning schools (hagwon). Unlike Korean Americans in their graduate programs, Korean Chinese students gain little status from being multilingual because English is usually not one of the languages they know. For some Korean Chinese, this is interpreted as another sign of South Korean closed-mindedness, which focuses solely on the West as the source of desirable cultural capital.

Better Global Citizens in the Future

Cosmopolitan Koreanness also gives Korean Americans and Korean Chinese a counternarrative for their experiences with marginalization as minorities growing up in the United States and China. As Annie points out, "America is just a bunch of people from other places; everyone has some sort of modifier. 'American' is what you are, but [hyphenated descriptors say] what kind of American you are." Jessica's story echoes a similarly positive spin on being Korean American. She is a twenty-eight-year-old Korean American woman who was born in Seoul and immigrated with her family to Virginia as an infant. She grew up in a "very ignorant little town" where she remembers her family as the only Asian immigrants who lived there. "Any racism that ever happened . . . is pure ignorance," such as the numerous times people assumed her family was Chinese, not Korean. Despite these experiences, Jessica says, "I felt American, actually, as soon as I became an American citizen. . . . I was a government teacher—civic duty and American duty, American identity; I really felt overly patriotic." Jessica sees being American as intrinsically linked to her identity as an immigrant. She continues, "American culture is fluid, enhanced every day by so many different experiences. Immigrant culture is a core part of American identity. I feel more American than anybody. . . . Immigrant society is America. I'm Korean on the surface, [but] it's just the surface, it's only an inch deep. If you get closer than that, under a microscope, I'm really nothing but American." The immigrant narrative central to the American Dream is proof that Korean Americans are the "real" Americans.

Many Korean Americans discover the economic advantages of being more "international" when they enter the job market. For example, before moving to South Korea, Jessica worked in Washington, DC, as a financial planner. She says, in that branch, "if you can't speak another language, you are looked down on. . . . The kid from Texas who is White and grew up there, he doesn't know another language. We called him Bubba"—she laughs—"'We have all this international jet set experience; why can't you fit in?'" She goes on to say that Americans who are born in the United States are "missing that component," signaling the racialized ways in which immigrants and children of immigrants have better access to the dominant narrative that the United States is a nation of immigrants. If cosmopolitanism is an embodied state that enables a certain disposition and competency to engage with a globalizing world, then bilingualism, biculturalism, and that "international jet set experience" allow racialized minorities like Korean Americans to increase their marketability over "Bubbas"—code for White, unhyphenated Americans—in the eyes of their prospective and current employers.

Interestingly, these statements occur within conversations in which these same people talk about the failures of multiculturalism, as discussed earlier, in chapter 1. In their formative years, assimilation was a desirable strategy to minimize their non-White racial identities. As children and teenagers, many Korean American respondents said avoided any kind of difference that marked them as "too Korean" to be American, such as accented English, "smelly" foods, or having "too many" Korean friends. Yet many, like Jessica, are aware of the increasing marketability of global citizenship in the contemporary labor market, particularly for young adults at the start of their professional careers. Her cultural and linguistic proficiency in Korean as well as her previous work experience at a large international firm are also what enabled her to get her previous job in Seoul. The very traits that were embarrassing or undesirable to Korean Americans as children have become assets in adulthood. Rather than a renewed commitment to their ethnic identity, return migration projects reveal another facet of Koreanness that provides value to Korean Americans as global citizens.

Just as Korean Americans use their immigrant histories and ethnic identities to claim the dispositions and competencies of embodied cosmopolitanism, Korean Chinese also see themselves as better global citizens than the dominant comparison group in China, ethnic Han. The combination of their cultural knowledge of Korean language, customs, and histories, their personal attachment to their Korean identities, their willingness to make short-term sacrifices in terms of migration debt and working difficult, dangerous, and dirty jobs give Korean Chinese access to employment in Seoul that ethnic Han largely do not have. Despite the initial high cost of international migration, higher wages and more job opportunities in Seoul translate into remittances, which in the long term, lead to greater economic mobility and better standards of living in China. With limited employment options in Northeast China, particularly in Yanbian Prefecture, and state policies that limit legal avenues for internal migration to larger cities, South Korea is a viable destination for many Korean Chinese.

For educational migrants, studying abroad is a common option because entry into graduate schools in more desired cities like Beijing and Shanghai is extremely competitive. For Korean Chinese in particular, Korean fluency as part of their global cultural capital makes graduate study in South Korea an option, one less accessible to ethnic Han in China. For example, Hee Sook is a third-generation Korean Chinese graduate student working toward a master's degree in early elementary education in Seoul. After she graduated from Peking University, one of the top schools in China, Hee Sook came to South Korea for graduate study because of its geographical closeness and her Korean cultural and linguistic fluency. However, she sees her move to Seoul as not solely about fulfilling her educational goals. She says that before she arrived, a Korean Chinese minister with whom she developed a close relationship in China encouraged her plans, telling her "You aren't Chinese, you are Korean." Affective ties to a strong Korean identity and already established paths to South Korea as a result of previous migrants translate into increased mobility for both Korean

Chinese labor and educational migrants, one of the hallmarks for global citizenship, over their ethnic Han counterparts.

With China's economic and political strength on the rise, some Korean Chinese have seen increased investment by South Korean businesses in China. This could translate into future employment prospects for Korean Chinese as cultural brokers and translators for South Korean firms looking for local contacts who could smooth out any challenges of doing business in China. In fact, some Korean Chinese note that more South Koreans are moving to China and there is a growing interest in learning Chinese "because the two will be interacting a lot in the future." Kyeong Mi points out that Korean Chinese who are fluent in Korean and Chinese gain an economic advantage over ethnic Han. She continues, "I think that as South Koreans come here, they'll incorporate Chinese culture into their lives and not be completely Korean or Chinese anymore." She believes the sustained relationship between South Korea and China could be the key to the survival of Korean Chinese communities and the emergence of a new hybridized South Korean culture.

Uneven Cosmopolitan Koreanness and Hierarchical Global Citizenship

"Don't ever forget you are Korean; you're not American." From her childhood, Maya says her dad repeated this over and over to her. Being told to take pride in Koreanness is something common to many Korean Americans and Korean Chinese in the study. It is, in part, a reason they have retained a strong attachment to their identities as Koreans even if they are second and third generation. But returns to South Korea offer something more—the ability to take pride in their transnational identities as global citizens. But the privileges of global citizenship are shaped by an individual's nation of origin and its status relative to South Korea in the global economy. In this case, the cosmopolitan cultural capital of Korean Americans consistently carries more weight than that of

Korean Chinese as evidenced in South Korean immigration policies and labor markets, as well as in everyday interactions.

Many Korean Americans are aware that favorable visa policies as well as economic opportunities related to their US citizenship and cultural capital facilitate their mobility in a global context. Matt is a soft-spoken man in his early thirties who has lived and worked in Asia for the past five years. He currently works as a lawyer at a company that runs one of the most popular social networking sites in South Korea. While Matt came to South Korea for the job opportunities, he sees his future as geographically open precisely because he is an American citizen. "If I want to live in Korea, I can choose to do that. If I want to live in America, then I can choose to do that. I'm definitely aware that I have a privileged status in [South] Korea simply due to the economic and political power of America." He continues, "I don't really place that much emphasis [on] whether I'm Korean or American or Korean American. Perhaps that's because all the choices are open for me because of the fact that I'm Korean American."

Matt, like many second-generation Korean American respondents, is on the F-4 visa discussed in chapter 2, which enables him to "do everything that a Korean citizen can do except vote," not to mention avoid the military service compulsory for all Korean adult men. Korean Chinese largely do not have this level of mobility. While a very small number of "Korean Chinese can claim [South Korean] citizenship if their parents or grandparents had citizenship," Kwang Soo notes that their situation in South Korea "is still incomparable to Korean Americans or Korean Japanese. The reason for this is because there is no equality or fairness in South Korean laws regarding those who live overseas." The unevenness of global citizenship means Korean Chinese are constantly aware of the more privileged diasporic return migrants like Korean Americans and Korean Japanese. In contrast, while Korean American respondents make references to many other diasporic communities from industrialized, core countries in South Korea like Japan, Canada, Sweden, and Australia, they make little, if any, mention of ethnic Koreans from China, Russia, or Latin America.

The Korean American educational migrants agree their American identities work in their favor in their graduate programs. For example, Grace is a twenty-six-year-old woman completing a master's degree in education at Seoul National University, one of the top universities in the country. Compared to some of the other international students, Grace says, "I think I've had an easier time. I've gained much more help than my peers because I'm an American." In fact, a few of her professors have occasionally sought out her help to edit their academic work for publication in English journals, which she feels is a sign of respect they have for her as a Korean American. Socially, it has not been difficult to befriend her South Korean classmates, which was not true for Korean Chinese respondents. Like Korean Americans who hope to use their work experiences in South Korea to further their competitiveness in the job market back in the United States, Grace sees her international graduate credentials as added capital for her as an aspiring academic. She has been accepted into a comparative international education graduate program at Stanford University and plans on using her professional networks cultivated in South Korea to further her future research agenda.

Korean Chinese graduate students, while mostly fluent in Korean, do not share similar stories of added status as international scholars. In fact, although they do not have concrete evidence to back their claims, they feel some professors grade Korean Chinese students harder compared to other international students. Even among their peers, they feel there is some social and professional discrimination because they are from China. Dong Moon, the Korean Chinese graduate student introduced earlier in the chapter, notes that US universities have more status in South Korea. For example, among the faculty at his graduate program, there are very few professors with educational credentials from Japan or China as compared to the United States. This may explain why his undergraduate degree from a very well-respected university in China goes largely unrecognized by his South Korean peers, who are more familiar with equivalent high-prestige US universities like Harvard, Princeton, and Yale. That said, earning advanced degrees in South Korea does give Korean Chinese more economic advantages and better employment opportunities back in China.

These inequalities enable and constrain the behaviors of return migrants while in South Korea. For example, many Korean Americans deliberately accentuate their Americanness as a display of power and superiority over South Koreans, especially at times when they feel vulnerable or threatened. An example is Herb's description of his altercation with a middle-aged South Korean man who cut in front of him to buy tickets at a subway station. When confronted, the man yelled at him in Korean and tried to push him out of the way. In response, Herb said, "I threw off his hand, I spoke to him in English, 'Don't touch me man.' He's cussing me out in Korean. I'm acting like I don't understand him. He's all like, 'Where are you from?'"—Herb uses a mocking tone in accented English—"I'm like, 'Where do you think I'm from? I'm from America. Get out of my face. . . . You want to fight?'" In the end, the South Korean man walked away angrily, deescalating a situation that could have become physical.

It would be a natural expectation that in South Korea, people should speak Korean in much the same way that immigrants in the US are told by nativists to speak English or "go back to where they came from." Herb is a foreigner in South Korea but despite this, his use of English and his imitation of the man's accented English illustrate the expectation that even in Seoul, being American is an identity of power that should be recognized. Many Korean Americans in the study tell me they engage in similar behaviors, such as purposely talking in English loudly on the subway, pretending not to understand Korean, or as women, smoking in public spaces in defiance of South Korean cultural norms. These subtle and direct actions are unmistakable displays of Americanness that make clear to those around them that they, as Korean Americans, are really Americans with higher global status and should not be expected to behave like Koreans even in South Korea.

Unlike Herb, Song Lim avoids any confrontations that might attract negative attention especially as an undocumented Korean Chinese resident in South Korea. An equivalent display of Chineseness as a status of power is largely absent in my conversations with Korean Chinese. In fact, the opposite appears to be more common. Many Korean Chinese say they deliberately try to "pass" in South Korea by softening their accents and consciously monitoring their behavior to minimize their visibility in risky situations. For Korean Chinese who have had their paychecks withheld or been subject to unfair treatment from employers or professors in their graduate programs, their response is largely to keep their heads down, keep working, and stay silent. This contrast highlights an important difference between the two communities of return migrants. Because Korean Americans are largely granted legal status by the South Korean state as members of the broader Korean family—as dongpo, as discussed in chapter 2—they are not as vulnerable as Korean Chinese.

Conclusion

Many Korean American and Korean Chinese return migrants in the study arrive in South Korea in search of a sense of belonging only to find themselves excluded as illegitimate ethnic subjects. Rather than strengthening their identities as Koreans, many invest in cultural and moral arguments that emphasize the differences between themselves and South Koreans. They do so by embracing characteristics of a cosmopolitan Koreanness that make them more mobile, more adaptable, and more open-minded global citizens. Korean Americans and Korean Chinese believe they possess the dispositions and competencies of cosmopolitanism outlined by Igarashi and Saito, giving them an advantage over South Koreans, and White Americans and Han Chinese, respectively. This strategy enables return migrants to claim a sense of belonging in South Korean society and legitimizes their decision to return to their homeland. Importantly, while cosmopolitanism confers certain privileges, it does so *when they are migrants*. Both Korean American and Korean Chinese respondents are more ambivalent about its enduring value once they return and settle down permanently in their home countries.

Conclusion
Finding Family among Foreigners

Let me put it this way, when you are in America, how
do people see you? . . . [as] Asian. When you come to Korea,
how do people see you? . . . [as] a foreigner. So no matter where
you are, you are a foreigner. . . . I've been trying to figure out
what it means to be Korean, what it means not to be Korean. In
America, I thought I was more Korean than I was because people
would make me out to be like that. When I came to Korea, in the
first couple months, I realized how very un-Korean I was. . . .
The longer I stay here, the more strong-willed I've become [in]
saying I'm not Korean.

Craig's words exemplify some of the key contradictions revealed
by return migrations. As someone who had very little contact with
South Korea until his return, Craig says he feels culturally "White"
but was always racialized as Asian in the United States. Although
he was born in South Korea and was adopted to a White family in
the Pacific Northwest as an infant, Craig feels like a foreigner
in Seoul, particularly because he understands very little Korean.
Labeled "Asian" (and thus not American) throughout his childhood and young adult life in the United States and "foreign"
during the years he has lived in South Korea, Craig is trapped

between the two; the mismatch between his national, racial, and ethnic identity follows him wherever he goes. Like Craig, Kwang Soo, a Korean Chinese man in his late thirties, feels similarly not quite Korean and not quite Chinese in both China and South Korea. His grandfather emigrated in 1927 from the Korean peninsula to China during the Japanese occupation. Over the past thirteen years, Kwang Soo has lived in South Korea working mostly as an undocumented labor migrant. He believes Korean Chinese "consider South Koreans to be dongpo, but South Koreans seem to think of Korean Chinese as foreigners. Chinese people have the same prejudice. They see Korean Chinese . . . as one of many national minorities who live in China."

Craig and Kwang Soo, like other Korean Americans and Korean Chinese in my study, have never and most likely will never cross paths with each other in Seoul. But if they did, I imagine the two would find they share many common perspectives on the knotty nature of "home" and "return." Koreanness is a multifaceted identity. At times, it is internally generated, immutable, and innate, as part of their "blood." At other times, it is externally imposed, an outcome of racial and ethnic logics that permanently mark them as foreigners. And as such, return migrants like Craig and Kwang Soo must constantly prove they are indeed "authentic" Koreans but also Americans or Chinese. Even though Craig possesses very little Korean cultural and linguistic fluency while Kwang Soo considers Korean his first language and primary identity, in South Korea, their Koreanness becomes equally scrutinized because of their citizenship.

Craig and Kwang Soo feel like foreigners at home and in their shared homeland. The key issue is that the "rules" of Koreanness are not consistent. From the macro politics of South Korean immigration policies and labor markets to the micro level of individual interactions and personal relationships, return migrants contend with constant, often conflicting messages about their social location within South Korean society—at times part of the larger Korean family and at other times foreigners. Markers such as gender and national citizenship matter greatly, as does their status as skilled and unskilled labor migrants or educational migrants.

Return migration is often reduced to the story of people searching for home in the homeland. There is an undeniably genuine emotional component for the women and men with whom I speak for why they moved to South Korea. As Myeong Dae puts it, "In my heart, I felt . . . it is the land of my ancestors. I thought I would hear Korean spoken whether I was awake or asleep and would feel more comfortable, and this is true." Led by his heart to the place of his ancestral roots, the familiar round tones of the Korean language reaffirm his roots to a country that treats him like a foreigner. Like Myeong Dae, many Korean Americans and Korean Chinese in the study come to South Korea because of more economic opportunities to improve their lives and the lives of their families. But they also sense the possibility of finding belonging and acceptance, something that eludes them at home. Like so many migrants who came before them, including their own families, mobility represents a way toward achieving these goals. But crossing national borders demands engagement with institutions that dictate who is a citizen, who has rights, who is legal, who is family, and who is foreign. This book highlights how these institutional decisions impose constraints on the daily lives of migrants and the ways they work around them.

I came to Seoul to investigate the questions posed in the introduction: Why do these Korean Americans and Korean Chinese move to South Korea? What are their economic, social, and cultural lives like in Seoul? How return migrants understand what does and does not "count" as Korean emerges out of countless quotidian moments from their lives in Seoul. Some attend daily Korean classes, struggling to learn a language that is both foreign and something they have heard their whole lives. Others, who are fluent, adapt their vocabulary and modulate their accents to fit in. Some have fallen in love and others have had their hearts broken. A few experience the joys of being popular and desired for the first time in their lives, while others feel incredibly isolated and lonely, separated from loved ones for years at a time. Some return migrants forge relationships with relatives they may have only known through pictures and stories from parents and grandparents. Others visit hometowns where their parents, grandparents, or even they themselves, were born and raised, and left so long ago. Some imagine a future in Seoul or making regular trips back, while others can't wait to go back home and never come back. Their experiences are incredibly varied, but one thing holds true: being Korean remains important.

I provide evidence of both the grounded and dynamic elements of Koreanness in a comparative analysis of two return migrant communities in South Korea. They negotiate narrow, uneven rules of ethnic exclusion and inclusion that alternately make them "family" through terms like "dongpo" and "minjok" or disregard them as "foreigners." I note how cultural criteria like food, language, customs, and practices that are quintessentially "Korean" along with existing ethnic and racial logics in each national context make Korean Americans and Korean Chinese "too foreign for home" despite the official commitment to multiculturalism and diversity espoused by both the US and Chinese states. These return migrants retrace the steps of their ancestors back to South Korea only to discover they fall short of true acceptance as Korean, based on criteria like blood, family, language proficiency, and general comportment. The returns teach them that they are "too foreign for here" as well. Their narratives shift toward a discourse of global citizenship and a cosmopolitan Koreanness only accessible to transnational actors like themselves. These return migrants used their hyphenated identities to elevate their own status in relation to multiple national reference points—South Korea, China, and the United States.

What are the consequences for those who are never enough for both home and homeland? Though many feel they are truly transnational and "float" between and across nations, the reality is that there is no institutional framework to uphold global citizenship. But even so, it becomes a powerful narrative to carve a space for "in-between" actors like themselves in the face of increased nationalism and growing hostility toward immigrants around the world. The return migration project offers a particular lens to filter memories of the past, engage with struggles in the present, and imagine possibilities in the future.

The Future of "Home" in between
Nationalism and Transnationalism

Can the children and grandchildren of immigrants ever achieve the full promise of citizenship in a single nation-state? Or will they always be nomads, moving from place to place in search of an "authentic" home? The ways ethnicity intersects with multiple axes of difference through the perspective of return migration provides important insights into the significance of citizenship and "home" in the twenty-first century. The continued migration of return migrants back and forth to the homeland presents an interesting challenge for policies geared toward diversity and multiculturalism within a specific nation's borders. Additional research on return migration projects could shed light on the direction different nations are taking toward members of the diaspora.

While multicultural nations like the United States and China preserve and celebrate diversity on the surface, the narratives of the Korean Americans and Korean Chinese in the study show that full membership as citizens remains elusive. In China, where the overwhelming majority of the population is ethnic Han, there are few benefits to sustained minority identities despite national policies that protect them. Korean Chinese are leaving Yanbian, their previously strong national minority educational systems are shutting down in the face of low enrollment, and families are divided as more and more children are left behind while adults migrate for economic opportunities. Beyond the third generation, the practical benefits of being fluent in Chinese culturally and linguistically outweigh sentimental attachments to Korean identities, especially as fewer and fewer adults perform traditional rituals and speak Korean. But politically, China's support for North Korea is weakening as they join with other nations like Japan, South Korea, and the United States to contain the threat its one-time ally poses to political stability in the region. Already, the Chinese government has tightened policies toward North Korean refugees in China, prosecuting any who provide aid and assistance to them. This disproportionately impacts Korean Chinese, who are concentrated in the border region and have had strong family ties to North Korean kin in the past.

As a result, it appears the Korean Chinese in this study see the future of Koreanness as dim. Most say Korean Chinese are more likely to identify as Chinese citizens in the future. Older Korean Chinese acknowledge the trend for younger generations to be more culturally and linguistically assimilated to mainstream Chinese society. This is the perspective of Song Soo, a second-generation Korean Chinese man, who says with some regret, "Korean Chinese will disappear completely. When you look at our cities in Yanbian, adults are disappearing, Korean Chinese schools are disappearing." Third- and later-generation Korean Chinese note that there is less resistance to outmarriage as compared to earlier generations. Many third-generation ethnics have already begun to lose their fluency in Korean, facilitated by the fact that Chinese is much more commonly used in the public sphere. From a practical standpoint, the consensus among Korean Chinese like Song Soo is that "Korean Chinese will just become Chinese," meaning ethnic drift may have been delayed but not prevented by official policies of multiculturalism.

The future of Koreanness in the United States appears to be following a similar path as that of Korean Chinese. But rather than becoming "just American," prevailing racial logics mean ethnic attachments will give way to racialized identities. While not the overwhelming numerical majority as ethnic Han in China, Whites and whiteness continues to be central to "American" values and culture. As a result, minoritized groups receive consistent messages that being non-White is a vulnerable status in the United States. Racism remains deeply embedded in legal institutions like law enforcement, the judicial system, and immigration policies and continues to be propagated by cultural institutions like the entertainment industry and news media. For Asian Americans, it means their continued absence in leading roles on television shows and movies except in stereotyped characters as foreigners, sidekicks, nerds, and social undesirables. It means being vulnerable to racial profiling—illustrated by the cases of Xi Xiaoxing and Wen Ho Lee, both US citizens falsely accused of espionage and arguably singled out because of their ancestral ties to China and Taiwan, respectively. In extreme cases like that of Anwar al-Awlaki, it means helplessly watching as the executive branch of the government approves measures to take the life of a US citizen deemed a credible threat to national security. History has shown that legal citizenship has offered little protection to Asian Americans, particularly in times of conflict and war. This underscores their status as "perpetual foreigners" who are always associated with their ancestral countries of origin regardless of generational status. This continues despite the celebration of diversity under multiculturalism paired with what sociologist Eduardo Bonilla-Silva calls "colorblind" discourse that promotes the ideology that we have moved "beyond" race.[1]

Reflecting on their ethnic future in the United States, many Korean Americans find commonalities with other Asian immigrant groups who have been subject to similar immigration policies and racialized into the same category. The salience of racial categories marks second- and later-generation Korean Americans as Asian Americans, but with each passing generation, many believe Koreanness itself will eventually become nonexistent. As Robert explains, "I wouldn't want to encourage Korean Americanness. . . . It's all turning American anyway, the whole world." He points to Japanese Americans who have "lost their ethnic language . . . and don't feel strongly associated to Japanese culture." Ironically, Asian Americans without significant ethnic ties would uphold part of the "safe" multiculturalism agenda by providing racial diversity without posing a threat to a common "American" culture based on whiteness.

Shifting the focus to ancestral homelands, how do return migrants and immigrants more broadly shape nationalism in countries like South Korea that promote a myth of racial and ethnic purity among its citizenry? In South Korea, changes are already occurring. Increased numbers of foreigners are settling permanently, the rates of international marriages are on the rise, and multiracial families are more visible. These immigrants are committed to improving their lives in their new home, as evidenced by activism for expanded and protected rights for migrant workers and calls for less restricted access to citizenship. Coethnics like Korean Chinese and Korean Americans who walk the line between foreign and family provide a test case for the elasticity of ethnicity. If current immigration policies continue to hold, "hierarchical nationhood" will continue to maintain inequalities within diaspora–homeland relations. In so doing, South Korea will continue to cultivate greater ties to and mobility for diasporic Koreans from wealthy, mostly Western nations in North America and Europe, as well as Japan, while discouraging relations with those from poorer or less strategically advantageous countries like China, Brazil, and Russia, which have small but significant communities of ethnic Koreans. As a consequence, future transnationalism and "global citizenship" may become a privilege of the already powerful, creating a new axis of inequality in Global North–South relations.

But can there be a different option for countries like South Korea that are in the process of transitioning into a fully multicultural society? In the case of South Korea, broadening the F-4 "family" visa offers the possibility of horizontal diasporic membership that would reduce the friction in border crossings and increase economic opportunities for all members of the Korean diaspora. Much of this depends on a loosening of South Korea's investment in a nationalism based on racial and ethnic purity and mitigating the fears that foreigners present to a national culture rooted in Koreanness. Additionally, while the possibility of reunification remains distant, it still shapes the narratives of some Korean Chinese, particularly those of the second generation. Should that come to fruition, it would have a dramatic impact on diasporic communities like Korean Chinese, whose ethnic ties to the peninsula have been largely dismissed in current geopolitics.

South Korea, as a homeland, needs the labor of diasporic actors like Korean Chinese and Korean Americans to maintain its strength as a nation. It also is reliant on their loyalty to remain the symbolic stronghold for all Koreans everywhere in the face of North Korea's claim to sovereignty. At the same time, the diaspora needs South Korea, as the original home of their ancestors and a symbolic place where they might truly belong and find acceptance unattainable in their countries of citizenship. Pragmatically, South Korea also depends on the military and political force of powerful allies like the United States and China to counter the rise of hostile actions by the North Korean government and keep "peace" on a divided peninsula still at war. The salience of ethnicity in the lives of second- and later-generation immigrants as evidenced by return migration projects means that certain kinds of migratory paths are preserved and facilitated, while others are closed off. Ultimately the relationships of diasporic communities to the homeland are dynamic, not fixed. During their return migration projects, Korean Chinese and Korean Americans do not "fall in love with Korea and Korean people and Korean culture," as Linda, a second-generation Korean American woman had hoped prior to her arrival in South Korea. Instead, returns reveal the logics and counterlogics of ethnic inclusion and exclusion—which variables add more value to Koreanness, which subtract from claims of legitimacy, which divide Koreans from non-Koreans, and which multiply the benefits of being simultaneously family and foreign in South Korea.

Acknowledgments

Writing a book is a long and painful process, and it has taken me over a decade from start to finish. First and foremost, my gratitude goes out to the Korean Americans and Korean Chinese who were willing to share their personal stories with a near stranger to give insight into their everyday lives as Koreans. I hope this book does justice to your experiences.

This project would never have existed without the encouragement and critical feedback from the members of my dissertation committee. Many thanks to John Mohr, Howard Winant, Carolyn Piñedo Turnovsky, and Diane Fujino, for your mentorship, advice, support, and gentle pushes to get me to the finish line of graduate school. Each of you have been an invaluable advisor, in both academia and outside matters, teaching me how to engage in critical scholarship, to hone my ideas, and most importantly to take ownership of and pride in my work even when I was floundering in self-doubt.

I was incredibly lucky to attend graduate school in a fertile place like the University of California, Santa Barbara, filled with inspiring sheroes and heroen, beautiful beaches, and delicious burritos. I am sincerely grateful to Carlos Alamo-Pastrana, Krista Bywater, Clayton Childress, Dana Collins, Joe Conti, Danielle and Pablo Hammack, Aki Hosoi, Michelle Jacob, LaShaune Johnson, Neda Maghbouleh, Moira O'Neil, Tony Samara, Anna Sandoval, and Molly Talcott. Thank you to the amazing staff at the MultiCultural Center, especially Zaveeni Khan-Marcus, Viviana Marsano, Patricia Machuca, Luniya Msuku, Rebekah Meredith, and so many student workers over the years for your camaraderie, encouragement, and for fiercely protecting a welcoming space for people of color on campus. I also am grateful to many colleagues at Dickinson College and in Carlisle, past and present, and special thanks to Suman Ambwani, Jennifer and Eric Schaefer, Susan Rose, and Tyson Smith. During my time in South Korea, special thanks to Sang-yeon Park, Patricia Seo, and my extended family, especially my cousin, Yoolim Lee. Thank you to Sherri Grasmuck for sponsoring me as a visiting scholar at Temple University during my sabbatical. Additional thanks to Lisa Banning at Rutgers University Press for advice and guidance as my editor through this process. I am grateful to Jane Yamashiro, Leslie Wang, and Mytoan Nguyen-Akbar for our conversations about Asian American homeland returns to Asia.

We can't write in a vacuum. Writing groups help ease the pain of sharing half-cooked work and overcome feelings of vulnerability in the face of critical feedback, especially when it is most needed! Many thanks to everyone who has read my work over the years, especially Mark Schuller, Karl Bryant, Hillary Haldane, Dan Schubert, Patricia van Leeuwaarde Moonsammy, Jerry Philogene, Shawn Bender, Light Carruyo, and Bob Ngo. I am indebted to my developmental editor, Sonal Nalkur, for her patience, her insightful feedback on many half-baked drafts, her constant support, and, most of all, for a dear friendship spanning two decades that has taken us well beyond our little room on the third floor of Donlon Hall. Here's to more adventures, both professional and personal—we will see the aurora borealis one day!

To Francesca Degiuli, Andrew, Bianca, and Giada Cammarano, I absolutely loved being the third, fourth, and eventually fifth wheel to your family for the last decade and a half. Francesca, one of the best chunkers in the world, I could not have made it through grad school and life beyond it without you. To Amy Steinbugler, my favorite jerk, your willingness to give smart, critical feedback at a moment's notice, your humor, and your constant belief in my work have meant everything to me. Much love to you, Erica, August, and Anika. Thank you to Sue and Robert, Katie, Erin,

Jude, and Maeve, and Melissa for always being supportive and welcoming me into the Love clan. Deepest gratitude to my parents, Hae Soon Lee and Hee Young Lee. You both have always given me the freedom to pursue my passion. I hope this book makes you proud. I'm grateful to my furry companions—Gabe, Riley, Victor, and Oliver—who have warmed my lap and my keyboard over the years. And to Erik Love, you have been my lifesaver when I was floundering in waves of self-doubt and helplessness. Thank you so much for your unconditional love and never-wavering faith over the past decade. I could not have finished this book without you. I love you and our big star, Aurora, right up to the moon and back.

Appendix A

Research Methods

This study is based on ethnographic and semistructured interview data with a total of sixty-four diasporic Korean return migrants from China and the United States over sixteen months of fieldwork in the Seoul metropolitan area. Thirty-three interviews were conducted with Korean Chinese, eighteen women and fifteen men, mostly second- and third-generation ethnic Koreans. The Korean Chinese sample was split between educational migrants and largely undocumented labor migrants who held low-wage jobs in the South Korean economy. Thirty-one interviews were with Korean Americans, eighteen women and thirteen men, all whom identified as 1.5- or second-generation Koreans in the United States. Unlike Korean Chinese, Korean Americans, whether educational or labor migrants or both, all had legal status in South Korea and held relatively high-wage white-collar jobs.

The majority of my contacts with Korean Chinese respondents were made through a church that houses a nongovernmental organization working on a diverse range of human rights issues, including challenges facing Korean Chinese workers in South Korea. The religious fellowship attracts a steady crowd of Korean Chinese, but they also frequent the church for other services including travel planning, legal assistance, access to prescription medications through a pharmacy staffed by South Korean volunteers every Sunday, haircuts, and dentistry, as well as low-cost meals downstairs in the kitchen/cafeteria and a short-term shelter for men and women. In addition to interviews, I conducted participant observations at regular rallies and events sponsored by the church. Eventually, I started offering biweekly English classes at the church, where I met many Korean Chinese workers and graduate students who participated in the study. Very quickly, I could see how Korean Chinese were much more complicated than the one-dimensional portrayal of them as uneducated, undocumented, and ultimately undesirable coethnic migrants.

Being a second-generation Korean American woman impacted the ways I approached the study as a researcher. My shared identity greatly facilitated contacts with Korean American return migrants and helped achieve a level of commonality between myself and my respondents. Many of the things they struggled with in Seoul were also aspects I could relate to myself. I recruited participants through posted advertisements on bulletin boards at two language schools based at the universities of Yonsei and Ewha. In addition, I advertised on two electronic message boards at two churches offering English services that were popular among Americans and other English-language speakers. I also used snowball sampling to recruit future participants and spent time with both communities in informal spaces such as restaurants, bars, and neighborhoods where they socialized and lived.

All of the Korean Chinese and Korean American respondents lived in the Seoul metropolitan area at the time I interviewed them. The goals of the in-depth interviews were to examine their motivations for moving to Seoul, how these diasporic Koreans understood what it meant to be Korean before they arrived, and how that understanding changed as a result of their return migration projects. I wanted to hear their stories of how and when they felt like they were embraced and rejected as Koreans by South Korea and their reactions to these interactions.

Appendix B

Characteristics of Respondents

TABLE B.1. Key characteristics of Korean American respondents

NAME	GENDER	AGE	GENERATIONAL STATUS	JOB/ OCCUPATIONAL FIELD	MARITAL STATUS
Jennifer	F	33	Second, born in US	Consultant, banking	Married, South Korean spouse
Catherine	F	23	Second, born in US	Rotary fellow/ graduate student	Single
Chun Ja	F	25	Second, born in SK, immigrated at age 5 (US green card holder)	English teacher, hagwon	White American partner
Gloria	F	26	Second, immigrated as an infant	SAT preparation teacher, hagwon & graduate student	Single
Connie	F	24	Second, born in US	Musician	Single
Heather	F	33	Second, born in SK, adopted to US	English teacher, college-level	Married, Korean American adoptee spouse
Jin Sook	F	35	Second, born in Japan, immigrated at about age 10	College counselor, high school	South Korean partner

(continued)

TABLE B.1. Key characteristics of Korean American respondents (*continued*)

NAME	GENDER	AGE	GENERATIONAL STATUS	JOB/ OCCUPATIONAL FIELD	MARITAL STATUS
Jessica	F	28	Second, born in SK, immigrated at age 1	Consultant, finance and banking	Divorced, currently single
Jin Ho	F	33	Second, born in SK, immigrated at age 8	English teacher, college-level	Married, South Korean spouse
Hye won	F	29	Second, born in US	English teacher, hagwon	Single
Linda	F	25	Second, born in US	SAT preparation teacher, hagwon	Single
Lydia	F	29	Second, born in SK, immigrated at age 9	Manager, investment management services	Single
Maya	F	Late 20s	Second, born in US	English teacher, hagwon, now voice-over actor	Single, South Korean partner
Paula	F	24	Second, born in US	English teacher, high school	Single
Annie	F	30	Second, born in SK, immigrated at age 2	Lawyer	Married, Korean American spouse
Sang Hee	F	31	1.5, born in SK, immigrated at age 17	Graduate student	White American partner
Sandra	F	61	First, born in SK, immigrated at age 18	Import/Export	Married, White American spouse
Min Ji	F	30	Second, born in SK, immigrated at age 5	Translation and editorial services	Single
Veronica	F	30	Second, born in SK, immigrated at age 11	English teacher, hagwon	Single

NAME	GENDER	AGE	GENERATIONAL STATUS	JOB/ OCCUPATIONAL FIELD	MARITAL STATUS
Adam	M	Early 20s	Second, born in US	Korean language student	Single
Craig	M	26	Second, born in SK, adopted to US	English conversation partner at SK firm, English textbook writer	Engaged, South Korean fiancée
Daniel	M	33	Second, born in SK, adopted to US	Graduate student	Married, White American spouse
Gabe	M	26	Second, born in US	US Air Force	Single
Gary	M	Mid-20s	Second, born in US	Korean language student	Single, Korean American partner
Herb	M	26	Second, born in US territory	English teacher, hagwon	Single
Jim	M	27	Second, born in US	English teacher, hagwon	Single
John	M	24	Second, born in SK, immigrated at age 1	English teacher, high school	Single
Matt	M	Mid-30s	1.5, born in SK, immigrated at age 8	Lawyer	Single
Nate	M	29	Second, born in US	English teacher, hagwon	Single
Peter	M	30	Second, born in US	Graduate student	Single
Robert	M	30	Second, born in US	Korean language student	Single
Sae Il	M	Late 20s	Second, born in US	Previously worked at a South Korean NGO	Single

TABLE B.2. Characteristics of Korean Chinese respondents

NAME	GENDER	AGE	GENERATIONAL STATUS	JOB/ OCCUPATIONAL FIELD	MARITAL STATUS
Kyeong Mi	F	29	Third	Graduate student	Single
Chung Ae	F	27	Third	Graduate student	Single
Hee Sook	F	Late 20s	Third	Graduate student	Single
Soon Hee	F	27	Third	Graduate student	Single
Mi Ja	F	Early 20s	Third	Graduate student	Single
Mi Ja's mother	F	Late 40s	Second	Currently unemployed	Married, Korean Chinese spouse
Eun Mi	F	Early 40s	Second	Domestic worker	Married, Korean Chinese spouse
Joon Young	F	26	Third	Graduate student	Single
Ok Hwa	F	Late 20s	Third	Graduate student	Single, South Korean partner
Hye Soon	F	57	Second	Domestic worker	Married, Korean Chinese spouse
Yu Na	F	46	Second	Domestic worker	Married, Korean Chinese spouse
Soo Young	F	Mid-30s	Third	Nursery	Single
Ji Yeon	F	32	Third	Clerk at mart	Single
Kyeong Won	F	37	Third	Import/Export	Single
Kang Hwa	F	31	Third	Currently unemployed	Married, Korean Chinese spouse
Woman 1*	F	N/A	Third	Graduate student	Single
Woman 2*	F	N/A	Third	Graduate student	Single
Woman 3*	F	N/A	Third	Graduate student	Single
Chul Mu	M	36	Second	NGO staff member	Married, South Korean spouse

NAME	GENDER	AGE	GENERATIONAL STATUS	JOB/ OCCUPATIONAL FIELD	MARITAL STATUS
Chang Hae	M	31	Third	Construction	Married, Korean Chinese spouse
Sung Bae	M	Mid-50s	Second	Currently unemployed,	Married, Korean Chinese spouse
Kwang Soo	M	Late 30s	Second	NGO staff member	Married, Korean Chinese spouse
Dong Moon	M	Late 20s	Third	Graduate student	Single
Song Lim	M	Mid-20s	Third	Interior construction	Single
Song Soo	M	Early 60s	Second	Currently unemployed, previously construction	Married, Korean Chinese spouse
Chul Soo	M	Late 30s/ Early 40s	Third	Manufacturing	Married, Korean Chinese spouse
Myeong Dae	M	32	Third	Manufacturing	Single
Man 1*	M	N/A	Second	Currently unemployed, previously construction	N/A
Man 2*	M	N/A	Second	Currently unemployed, previously manufacturing	N/A
Man 3*	M	N/A	Second	Currently unemployed	N/A
Man 4*	M	N/A	Third	Graduate student	Single
Man 5*	M	N/A	Second	Currently unemployed	N/A
Man 6*	M	N/A	Second	Currently unemployed	N/A

* Declined to state name or other identifying characteristics

Notes

Introduction

1. All names are pseudonyms to protect the confidentiality of research participants. The assigned Anglicized or Korean name reflects that of the original.

2. It is perhaps unsurprising that most of my social outings with South Koreans lasted until the early hours of the morning. This is an adjustment for many Korean Americans who discover that no matter how late the evening goes with colleagues and superiors, even on a weekday, they are still expected at work at the usual time the next morning.

3. Steven Denney, "South Korea's Migrant Workers in the Public Eye," *Diplomat*, September 10, 2015, http://thediplomat.com/2015/09/south -koreas-migrant-workers-in-the-public-eye/.

4. Many thanks to Sonal Nalkur for this term.

5. A. Christou and R. King, *Counter-Diaspora*, 2014.

6. F. Saussure, "General Linguistics," 1916/1974.

7. M. Seigel, "Beyond Compare," 2005.

8. Ibid., 66.

9. N. Glick Schiller, L. Basch, and C. Blanc-Szanton, "Transnationalism," 1992.

10. B. Anderson, "Imagined Communities," 1983.

11. For example, R. King and A. Christou ("Reverse Transnationalism," 2011) and R. King, A. Christou, and J. Ahrens ("'Diverse Mobilities,'" 2011) find that second-generation Greek German and Greek American returnees struggle to integrate into a modern Greek society that does not wholly embrace them as "hyphenated Greeks" despite the fact that

many grew up with very strong affective ties to Greece and their Greek identities.

12. On Japanese Brazilians, see J. H. Roth (*Brokered Homeland*, 2002) and T. Tsuda (*Ethnic Homeland*, 2003); on Indian Americans in India, see S. Jain ("Love and Money," 2013); on Vietnamese Americans in Vietnam, see M. Nguyen-Akbar ("Tensions of Diasporic 'Return' Migration," 2014); on Chinese Americans in China, see L. Wang ("The Benefits of In-betweenness," 2016); on Japanese Americans in Japan, see J. H. Yamashiro (*Constructing Japanese American Identity*, 2017).

13. See A. Louie ("Creating Histories," 2002; *Chineseness across Borders*, 2004) on returns of Chinese Americans to China, B. Fehler ("(Re) constructing Roots," 2011) on returns of African Americans to Ghana, and R. King, A. Christou, and J. Ahrens ("'Diverse Mobilities,'" 2011) on returns of second-generation Greek Germans to Greece.

1. Premigration Condition

1. R. Alba and V. Nee, "American Mainstream," 2003.
2. R. Park, *Race and Culture*, 1950.
3. A. Greeley, *Why Can't They?*, 1971.
4. P. Kasinitz, "Herbert Gans," 2014.
5. H. Gans, "Symbolic Ethnicity," 1999.
6. S. Lieberson and M. Waters, "From Many Strands," 1988.
7. C. Lee, *China's Korean Minority*, 1986.
8. W. Choi, "Korean Minority," 2001. Evidence of Korean Chinese support for Korean nationalism and anti-Japanese sentiment can be found in their significant literary contributions beginning in the 1900s in poetry, fiction, and dramas. See C. Piao ("Yanbian Korean," 1990), S. Masayuki ("Korean National Liberation," 1990), J. Kim (*Contested Embrace*, 2016), and E. Han (*Contestation and Adaptation*, 2013) for more information on the early histories of Korean Chinese communities.
9. C. Piao, "Yanbian Korean," 1990; A. Schmid, *Korea between Empires*, 2002; B. Cumings, *Korea's Place*, 1997.
10. P. G. Min, "Comparison of Korean Minorities," 1992.
11. S. Jin, "Rights of Minority Nationalities," 1990.

12. P. G. Min, "Koreans to United States," 2013.

13. E. Kim, *Adopted Territories*, 2010.

14. E. J. W. Park and J. S. W. Park, *Probationary Americans*, 2005.

15. P. G. Min, "Koreans to United States," 2013.

16. Ibid.

17. P. G. Min and C. Kim, "Growth and Settlement," 2013.

18. "Chuseok" is an important Korean harvest festival, and "seolnal" is the first day of the lunar calendar akin to New Year's Day.

19. J. He, "China's Policy on Nationalities," 1990, 3.

20. W. Choi, "Korean Minority," 2001.

21. T. Heberer, *China and National Minorities*, 1989, 40.

22. E. Han, *Contestation and Adaptation*, 2013.

23. F. Dikotter, "Culture, 'Race' and Nation," 1996.

24. Much has been written on various national minority groups in China. See E. Han, *Contestation and Adaptation*, 2013; T. Heberer, *China and National Minorities*, 1989; C. Mackerras, *China's Minority Cultures*, 1995; S. White, "Gendered Naxi Identities," 1998; Safran, *Nationalism and Ethnoregional Identities*, 1998; H. Schwarz, *Minorities of Northern China*, 1984; E. Hannum and Y. Xie, "Ethnic Stratification," 1998.

25. W. Choi, "Korean Minority," 2001.

26. C. Mackerras, *China's Minority Cultures*, 1995.

27. C. Piao, "Yanbian Korean," 1990.

28. E. Han, *Contestation and Adaptation*, 2013.

29. Ibid., 85.

30. Korean Chinese generally used the word "minjok" in conversation, which does not have an exact translation in English. While in South Korea, this term carried familial overtones, when used to refer to the Chinese context, it had cultural and ethnic connotations.

31. Also known as "Yanji," in China's Jilin Province.

32. S. J. Kim, "Economic Status and Role," 2003.

33. E. Han, *Contestation and Adaptation*, 2013, 74.

34. Some scholars argue that differences between rural and urban Chinese are distinct enough to create deep inequalities between Chinese citizens. For example, Dorothy J. Solinger ("China's Internal Migration," 1990), in her work on Chinese internal migration, found that "urban Chinese

generally view rural Chinese as ethnically distinct" (456). For more on these disparities, see K. D. Roberts, "China's 'Tidal Wave,'" 1997, and X. Wu and D. Treiman, "Household Registration System," 2004.

35. K. D. Roberts, "China's 'Tidal Wave,'" 1997.

36. For migrant laborers who do not secure legal permission, their status is reduced to that of undocumented migrant workers regardless of their Chinese citizenship. They are subject to lower wages as well as harassment from authorities. Following economic reforms that began in the 1980s, there has been a slight loosening of restrictions, freeing up some rural-to-urban migration, but these workers face discrimination in the labor market as well as the housing sector as compared to registered urban residents.

37. Philip Bump, "Donald Trump's Plan to Bar Muslim Immigrants from Entering the United States, Annotated," *Fix*, August 15, 2016, https://www.washingtonpost.com/news/the-fix/wp/2016/08/15/donald-trumps-plan-to-bar-immigrants-from-entering-the-united-states-annotated/.

38. Y. L. Espiritu, *Labor, Laws and Love*, 2000, 21.

39. M. Tuan, *Forever Foreigners*, 2005.

40. M. Das Gupta, "What Is Indian," 1997.

41. V. Prashad, *Karma of Brown Folk*, 2000.

42. It is also noteworthy that, in 2010, Arizona also passed SB 1070, in which law enforcement is allowed to stop an individual based on "reasonable suspicion" of undocumented status. Failure to provide documentation when requested is considered a misdemeanor crime. Critics argued that enforcement of this law disproportionately targeted non-White communities, particularly Latino communities, in areas near the US–Mexico border, based on the racialized assumption that non-White meant "not American."

43. Racism inherent in the legislation discussed above becomes difficult to prove because they are framed as neutral initiatives to improve outcomes for "our" children or safety in "our" neighborhoods even as they make vulnerable certain communities of color and immigrant communities. These laws had clearly racialized consequences, yet the laws themselves are worded using a race-neutral discourse that avoided any explicit mention of race or ethnicity. Sociologist Eduardo Bonilla-Silva (*Racism without Racists*, 2003) argues that "colorblind" language facilitates what he calls, "colorblind racism" in which "racism" is reduced to its most

extreme forms such as White supremacist groups like the KKK or obsolete structures like slavery from the distant past.

44. S. Lieberson and M. Waters, "From Many Strands," 1988.

45. I use quotes to signal that in many states, like California and Hawai'i, non-White communities have surpassed or are projected to pass Whites as the majority population.

46. P. G. Min, *Caught in the Middle*, 1996.

47. C. J. Kim, *Bitter Fruit*, 2000; P. G. Min, *Caught in the Middle*, 1996; N. Abelmann and J. Lie, *Blue Dreams*, 1995.

48. C. J. Kim, *Bitter Fruit*, 2000; P. G. Min, *Caught in the Middle*, 1996.

49. I never heard the term "FOB" used in reference to older immigrants, such as parents or anyone from their parents' generation, who often engaged in these behaviors. "FOB" is directed mainly towards younger, 1.5- or second-generation Korean Americans.

50. In their study of identity in ethnic Chinese living in Singapore, C. Tong and K. Chan ("One Face, Many Masks," 2001) found that in interviews, Chinese-educated respondents used the term "banana" as a pejorative term to refer to English-educated ethnic Chinese who are seen to have lost their roots to cultural assimilation.

2. Return Migrants in the South Korean Immigration System and Labor Market

1. The terms "dongpo" and "gyopo" can both be used in reference to ethnic Koreans living outside of the Korean peninsula who share the same ancestry. The former is said to have more inclusive implications, referring to all overseas Korean communities, while the latter has a more narrow interpretation linked to South Korean nationalism rather than the Korean peninsula more broadly. Generally speaking, gyopo then only refers to overseas Americans, excluding Korean Chinese. No Korean Chinese used the term "gyopo" in conversation with me. Instead, most talked about dongpo or minjok—the latter loosely translates to "nation," "race of people," or "ethnic group" with shared bloodlines.

2. D. H. Seol and J. Skrentny, "Ethnic Return Migration," 2009, 161, 166.

3. H. R. Park, "Narratives of Migration," 1996; J. S. Park and P. Y. Chang, "Global Korean Community," 2005.

4. D. H. Seol and J. Skrentny, "Ethnic Return Migration," 2009, 151.

5. J. S. Choi and S. Choi, "Social work intervention," 2005; K. Gray "Migrant Labor," 2006; A. E. Kim and G. S. Park, "Nationalism, Confucianism," 2003; T. Lim "Political Activism," 2003; K. H. S. Moon, "Strangers in the Midst," 2000; H. R. Park, "Narratives of Migration," 1996; I. Pirie, "Social Injustice," 2006.

6. According to the 2015 rankings of countries by gross domestic product released by the World Bank. "Gross Domestic Product 2015," World Bank, April 28, 2017, http://databank.worldbank.org/data/download/GDP.pdf.

7. Korea Labor Foundation, "Statistics Korea Has Released the Results of the '2012 Foreign Residents Employment Survey,'" November 30, 2011, last modified December 5, 2012, http://www.migrantok.org/english/viewtopic.php?popup=yes&today=no&printable=yes&t=637&postdays=0&postorder=desc&start=0.

8. Ibid.

9. Refers to the "Scholastic Aptitude Test" or the "Scholastic Assessment Test," a standardized test commonly used in the United States for college and university admissions.

10. Refers to the "Test of English as a Foreign Language," a standardized test for English-language proficiency often used in US college admissions for applicants who are not native English speakers.

11. Refers to "American College Testing," a standardized test used in US college admissions as an alternative to the SAT.

12. Interviews with Korean Americans were all conducted in English. Korean words included in any of the conversations are taken from the original quote.

13. "2013 Foreign Labour Force Survey," Statistics Korea, November 7, 2013, http://kostat.go.kr/portal/eng/pressReleases/5/3/index.board?bmode=read&aSeq=310276&pageNo=&rowNum=10&amSeq=&sTarget=&sTxt=.

14. Gray ("Migrant Labor," 2006) notes that the Industrial Trainee System (ITS) was enacted in 1994 to regulate and delineate the rights of foreign migrant workers. As a result of grassroots organizing and protests by NGOs and religious groups on behalf of irregular South Korean workers and temporary foreign workers, the ITS was replaced in 1996 with the

Labor Permit System (LPS). However this was met with opposition from many South Korean small and medium businesses, and under the Kim Dae Jung administration, the Employment Permit System (EPS) was proposed. The ITS and EPS operated simultaneously, with plans for the ITS to be eliminated by 2007. Most of the interviews with Korean Chinese in this book took place in 2005, during a time of much transition. As a result, it is often unclear under which system these "trainees" entered, even to the workers themselves. The EPS was reformed in 2007 to extend term limits from three to five years and increased mobility in employment without loss of legal status, but it was not in place at the time of the interviews.

15. T. Lim "Political Activism," 2003; K. H. S. Moon "Strangers in the Midst," 2000.

16. J. S. Choi and S. Choi, "Social work intervention," 2005; K. H. S. Moon, "Strangers in the Midst," 2000; T. Lim "Political Activism," 2003; H. R. Park "Narratives of Migration," 1996.

17. J. S. Choi and S. Choi, "Social work intervention," 2005.

18. Korea Labor Foundation, "Statistics Korea Has Released."

19. Equivalent to about $9,300 US dollars.

20. As noted earlier, "gyopo" is a contemporary, politicized term that applies only to descendants of former South Korean citizens and, as a result, is generally used in reference to ethnic Koreans in North America, Japan, and Europe rather than Russia and China. This is different from "dongpo" which has a broader connotation of "overseas Koreans with ties to the Korean peninsula."

21. "2013 Foreign Labour Force Survey," Statistics Korea.

22. This is difficult for some Korean Americans, particularly adoptees, who are often not recorded on these registries.

23. South Korea has long held the top spot for longest working hours among industrialized countries.

24. Room salons are often talked about by Korean Americans as establishments that employ South Korean women to serve drinks and dance with customers. There is a strong assumption that paid sex work might also be procured. I cannot confirm these claims independently, but room salons come up multiple times in conversations with Korean Americans.

25. Some notable examples are the 2001 Enron scandal; Bernie Madoff who, in 2009, was convicted of financial fraud on a level previously unseen; and the subprime mortgage crisis in 2007–9.

26. For in-depth ethnographic studies on domestic work focusing on Mexican and Central American domestic workers in the United States, see P. Hondagneu-Sotelo (*Doméstica*, 2001), M. Romero (*Maid in the U.S.A.*, 2002), and G. Chang (*Disposable Domestics*, 2000), among many others. R. Parreñas (*Servants of Globalization*, 2001) looks at the experiences of Filipina domestic workers and nannies in the United States and Italy.

27. A visible example of this took place in January of 1995 when a coalition of South Korean NGOs, trade unions, religious organizations, and migrant rights organizations staged a public protest at Myeongdong Cathedral to expose egregious labor practices including withholding of wages, violence, abuse, and the confiscation of passports by South Korean employees.

28. "Korean Korean" is commonly used by Korean Americans as a way to refer to South Koreans. It is perhaps a carryover from the US in which modifiers are used in front of American to signify ethnic and/or racial identities.

29. "Joseon" is the historical term referring to the Korean peninsula. Rather than the Korean terms for South Korea (hanguk) and North Korea (eebuk or bukhan), Korean Chinese generally used "Joseon" when they talked about Korea as a homeland.

3. Of "Kings" and "Lepers": The Gendered Logics of Koreanness in the Social Lives of Korean Americans

1. A. Hochschild, *Second Shift*, 1989, 15.

2. One example discussed is an "upstairs/downstairs" division of responsibilities within the home so that the husband maintains the upstairs areas and the wife the downstairs spaces. While on the surface, this agreement seems equitable, the amount of labor within these two spaces differed significantly because the majority of common spaces that are used more frequently including the kitchen are "downstairs." As a result, this couple preserved unequal gender relations in the family.

3. M. Kimmel "Masculinity as Homophobia," 1994; M. Messner, *Power at Play*, 1992; R. W. Connell, *Masculinities*, 2005.

4. M. Kimmel "Masculinity as Homophobia," 1994; R. W. Connell, *Masculinities*, 2005.

5. P. H. Collins, *Black Feminist Thought*, 1990.

6. Ibid., 68.

7. Y. L. Espiritu, *Labor, Laws and Love*, 2000, 87.

8. The hashtag #starringjohncho started on the social networking site Twitter campaigns Hollywood for more roles for Asian American leading men. It superimposes the face of John Cho, a Korean American actor, as the lead in many popular adventure and romantic movies. There is also a website: http://starringjohncho.com/.

9. A. Lu and Y. J. Wong, "Stressful Experiences of Masculinity," 2013.

10. D. Iwamoto, L. Liao and W. Kiu "Masculine Norms," 2010; Y. L. Shek, "Asian American Masculinity," 2006; S. J. Lee, "Hmong American Masculinities," 2004; A. Chen, "Lives at the Periphery," 1999; P. Chua and D. C. Fujino, "Negotiating New Masculinities," 1999.

11. This is clearly illustrated in an article in a 2004 issue of the US men's magazine, Details, with the headline, "Gay or Asian?" above an Asian American male model.

12. As discussed in the previous chapter, these are private learning centers or cram schools, for extra tutoring or lessons outside of school, where many Korean Americans find employment.

13. Hondagneu-Sotelo and Messner, "Gender Displays, Men's Power," 1994; M. Kaufman, "Experiences of Power," 1994; H. Brod, "Some Masculinities," 1994.

14. A. Chen, "Lives at the Periphery," 1999.

15. Andrew Ross Sorkin, "An E-Mail Boast to Friends Puts Executive Out of Work," *New York Times*, May 22, 2001, last modified May 23, 2001, http://www.nytimes.com/2001/05/22/business/22MAIL.html.

16. "Jemi gyopo" is used to refer to Korean Americans in South Korea.

17. While I do not directly ask about their sexual orientation, in conversation around sexuality and relationships, Korean American men nearly always assume a heterosexual norm.

18. Amerasian is used to refer to multiracial Koreans, particularly (but not exclusively) products of relationships between US GIs and South Korean women.

19. The first celebrates the new year according to the lunar calendar. The second is a major holiday commemorating the harvest (chuseok), which is roughly the South Korean version of US Thanksgiving.

20. In *The Second Shift: Working Parents and the Revolution at Home*, A. Hochschild and Machung's examination of the division of reproductive labor among couples found that women are almost always responsible for the "second shift"—the work needed to keep a household functioning smoothly—even if they worked a full "shift" outside of the home.

21. Statistics provide some empirical evidence for this assertion. A 2014 OECD survey found that just over 27 percent of the female workforce engaged in part-time work, well above the average of 12.5 percent among twenty-two OECD countries. While the overall numbers of South Korean women in the workforce has increased dramatically in the last few decades, it appears that many quit their jobs, often after getting married and/or having children. Some later return to part-time work but very few to full-time work. "OECD Economic Surveys Korea," OECD, June 2014, https://www.oecd.org/eco/surveys/Overview_Korea_2014.pdf.

22. K. Pyke and D. Johnson, "Racialized Femininities," 2003.

23. I. Padavic and B. Reskin, *Women and Men at Work*, 1994; C. MacKinnon, *Feminist Theory of State*, 1989; A. Hochschild and Machung, *Second Shift*, 1989.

24. "Player" is a slang term used primarily for men (although it can be applied to women) who have "game," meaning they are generally charismatic and charming, able to date many people at once.

25. As noted elsewhere, the label "Korean Korean" is a commonly used one by Korean Americans to denote South Korean.

26. While Korean American men smoked outside on the streets, none of them mentioned any harassment while doing so. During my sixteen months of fieldwork, it was a rare sight to see a woman of any race or ethnic background smoking in public. Exceptions were in areas popular among foreigners, including Itaewon, a district immediately outside of the US Yongsan military base, and Sinchon and Hongdae, neighborhoods near the universities of Ewha, Yonsei, and Hongik.

4. "Aren't We All the People of Joseon?": Claiming Ethnic Inclusion through History and Culture

1. G. Shin, J. Freda and G. Yi, "Politics of Ethnic Nationalism," 1999, 469.
2. G. Shin, *Ethnic Nationalism in Korea*, 2006, 2.
3. A. Schmid, *Korea between Empires*, 2002.
4. J. H. Roth, *Brokered Homeland*, 2002; T. Tsuda, *Ethnic Homeland*, 2003.
5. As discussed in chapter 2, the F-4 visa is open only to direct descendants of former South Korean citizens and, as such, is largely unavailable to Korean Chinese, whose families emigrated prior to the establishment of South Korea.
6. Examples of counting words in English are "sheets" of paper, "flock" of geese or "cups" of coffee.
7. In an odd way, this parallels the FOB–twinkie debate discussed in chapter 1. In that context, certain Korean Americans are criticized by their Korean American peers for being "too Korean" in their behaviors and social networks, while other are penalized for being "too Westernized" and losing touch with their Korean roots. Korean Chinese saw the retention of Korean culture and language as desirable, whereas this is seen by Korean Americans as a negative characteristic of "FOBs" in the US. From the perspective of Korean Chinese, South Koreans might be in danger of becoming "twinkies"!
8. G. Shin, J. Freda and G. Yi, "Politics of Ethnic Nationalism," 1999.
9. There are an estimated 140,000 to 200,000 North Koreans hiding in China (B. Chung, "Between Defector and Migrants," 2008). Korean Chinese concentrated in this border area work towards protecting North Koreans from discovery and subsequent repatriation to North Korea, where they would face severe punishments including assignment to political prison camps or even death. The relationship between North Koreans and Korean Chinese is not always a positive one. There have been reports of sex trafficking of North Korean women defectors by Korean Chinese or forced marriages of these women to Korean Chinese men. Additionally, the Chinese state has increased security measures along its border with North Korea and cracked down more intensely on the presence of North Koreans in China.
10. "*Talbukja*" is a term used to refer to North Koreans in South Korea that carries some negative connotations, such as "refugee" or "fugitive." A

newer term, *saetomin*, has been proposed, which emphasizes their status as "migrants," though none of the Korean Chinese I speak with use this in reference to North Koreans.

11. B. Chung, "Between Defector and Migrants," 2008.
12. Ibid.
13. Ibid., 3.
14. T. Tsuda, *Ethnic Homeland*, 2003, 192.
15. Some examples within Seoul include Itaewon in Yongsan-gu, the highly Westernized commercial and residential district bordering the US military garrison Yongsan, visibly marked by the strong presence of soldiers, tourists, and foreigners in general, and Gangnam-gu, a district south of the Han River generally known for high real estate prices and concentrated wealth (akin to Beverly Hills in Southern California) where many well-to-do South Koreans live. In 2012, South Korean performer Psy released a widely popular music video, "Gangnam Style," that slyly critiqued the consumerist lifestyle in this neighborhood.
16. This is similar to "Konglish" used by Korean Americans, although that generally means the occasional Korean term used in an English sentence. However, in the case of Korean Americans, many stated that while their parents generally used Korean to talk to them, their replies would often be in English.
17. J. H. Yamashiro, *Constructing Japanese American Identity*, 2017, 149.
18. Ibid.

5. The Logics of Cosmopolitan Koreanness and Global Citizenship

1. A. Christou and R. King, *Counter-Diaspora*, 2014.
2. U. Hannerz, "Cosmopolitans and Locals," 1990, 239.
3. Ibid.
4. Ibid., 239.
5. H. Igarashi and H. Saito, "Cosmopolitanism as Cultural Capital," 2014, 225.

Conclusion

1. E. Bonilla-Silva, *Racism without Racists*, 2003.

References

Abelmann, Nancy, and John Lie. 1995. *Blue Dreams: Korean Americans and the Los Angeles Riots*. Cambridge, MA: Harvard University Press.

Alba, Richard, and Victor Nee. 2003. "Remaking the American Mainstream: Assimilation and Contemporary Immigration," *International Review of Modern Sociology* 33:269–71.

Anderson, Benedict. 1983. *Imagined Communities: Reflections on the Origin and Spread of Nationalism*. London: Verso Press.

Bhabha, Homi. 1994. *The Location of Culture*. London: Routledge.

Bonilla-Silva, Eduardo. 2003. *Racism without Racists: Color-Blind Racism and the Persistence of Racial Inequality in the United States*. New York: Roman & Littlefield.

Brod, Harry. 1994. "Some Thoughts on Some Histories of Some Masculinities: Jews and Other Others," in *Theorizing Masculinities*, edited by Harry Brod and Michael Kaufman, 82–96. Thousand Oaks, CA: Sage Publications.

Chang, Grace. 2000. *Disposable Domestics: Immigrant Women Workers in the Global Economy*. Cambridge, MA: South End Press.

Chen, Anthony. 1999. "Lives at the Center of the Periphery, Lives at the Periphery of the Center: Chinese American Masculinities and Bargaining with Hegemony," *Gender & Society* 13:584–607.

Choi, Jae-Sung, and Soochan Choi. 2005. "Social Work Intervention with Migrant Workers in South Korea: Micro and Macro Approaches," *International Social Work* 48:655–65.

Choi, Woo-Gil. 2001. "The Korean Minority in China: The Change of its Identity," *Development and Society* 30:119–41.

Christou, Anastasia, and Russell King. 2014. *Counter-Diaspora: The Greek Second Generation Returns "Home."* Cambridge, MA: Harvard University Press.

Chua, Peter, and Diane C. Fujino. 1999. "Negotiating New Asian-American Masculinities: Attitudes and Gender Expectations," *Journal of Men's Studies* 7:391–413.

Chung, Byung-Ho. 2008. "Between Defector and Migrants: Identities and Strategies of North Koreans in South Korea," *Korean Studies* 21:1–27.

Collins, Patricia Hill. 1990. *Black Feminist Thought: Knowledge, Consciousness, and the Politics of Empowerment*. New York: Routledge.

Connell, R. W. 2005. *Masculinities*. 2nd ed. Berkeley: University of California Press.

Cumings, Bruce. 1997. *Korea's Place in the Sun: A Modern History*. New York: W. W. Norton & Company.

Das Gupta, Monisha. 1997. "What Is Indian about You? A Gendered, Transnational Approach to Ethnicity," *Gender & Society* 11:591.

Dikotter, Frank. 1996. "Culture, 'Race' and Nation: The Formation of National Identity in Twentieth Century China," *Journal of International Affairs* 49:598.

Espiritu, Yen Le. 2000. *Asian American Women and Men: Labor, Laws and Love*. New York: Altamira Press.

Fehler, Benedicte. 2011. "(Re)constructing Roots: Genetics and the 'Return' of African Americans to Ghana," *Mobilities* 6:585–600.

Gans, Herbert. 1999. "Symbolic Ethnicity: The Future of Ethnic Groups & Cultures in America," in *Making Sense of America: Sociological Analyses and Essays*, edited by Herbert Gans, 167–202. Lanham, MD: Rowman & Littlefield.

Glick Schiller, Nina, Linda Basch, and Cristina Blanc-Szanton. 1992. "Transnationalism: A New Analytic Framework for Understanding Migration," *Annals of the New York Academy of Sciences* 645:1–24.

Gray, Kevin. 2006. "Migrant Labor and Civil Society Relations in South Korea," *Asian and Pacific Migration Journal* 15:381–90.

Greeley, Andrew. 1971. *Why Can't They Be like Us? America's White Ethnic Groups*. New York: E. P. Dutton.

Hall, Stuart. 1990. "Cultural Identity and Diaspora," in *Identity: Community, Culture, Difference*, edited by J. Rutherford, 222–37. London: Lawrence & Wishart.

Han, Enze. 2013. *Contestation and Adaptation: The Politics of National Identity in China*. Oxford: Oxford University Press.

Hannerz, Ulf. 1990. "Cosmopolitans and Locals in World Culture," *Theory, Culture & Society* 7:239.

Hannum, Emily, and Yu Xie. 1998. "Ethnic Stratification in Northwest China: Occupational Differences between Han Chinese and National Minorities in Xinjiang, 1982–1990," *Demography* 35(3):323–33.

He, Jiancheng. 1990. "China's Policy on Nationalities," in *Koreans in China*, edited by Dae-Sook Suh and Edward J. Shultz, 1–20. Honolulu: Center for Korean Studies, University of Hawaii.

Heberer, Thomas. 1989. *China and Its National Minorities: Autonomy or Assimilation?* London: East Gate Books.

Hochschild, Arlie. 1989. *Second Shift: Working Parents and the Revolution at Home.* New York: Penguin Books.

Hondagneu-Sotelo, Pierrette. 2001. *Doméstica: Immigrant Workers Cleaning and Caring in the Shadows of Affluence.* Berkeley: University of California Press.

Hondagneu-Sotelo, Pierrette and Michael Messner. 1994. "Gender Displays and Men's Power," in *Theorizing Masculinities*, edited by Harry Brod and Michael Kaufman, 200–218. Thousand Oaks, CA: Sage Publications.

Igarashi, Hiroki, and Hiro Saito. 2014. "Cosmopolitanism as Cultural Capital: Exploring the Intersection of Globalization, Education and Stratification," *Cultural Sociology* 8:222–39.

Iwamoto, D., L. Liao, and W. Kiu. 2010. "Masculine Norms, Avoidant Coping, Asian Values and Depression among Asian American Men," *Psychology of Men & Masculinity* 11:15–24.

Jain, Sonali. 2013. "For Love and Money: Second-Generation Indian-Americans 'Return' to India," *Ethnic and Racial Studies* 36:896–914.

Jin, Shangzhen. 1990. "The Rights of Minority Nationalities in China: The Case of the Yanbian Korean Autonomous Prefecture," in *Koreans in China*, edited by Dae-Sook Suh and Edward J. Shultz, 31–43. Honolulu: Center for Korean Studies, University of Hawaii.

Kasinitz, Philip. 2014. "Herbert Gans and the Death of Miss Norway," *Ethnic and Racial Studies* 37:772.

Kaufman, Michael. 1994. "Men, Feminism, and Men's Contradictory Experiences of Power," in *Theorizing Masculinities*, edited by Harry Brod and Michael Kaufman, 142–64. Thousand Oaks, CA: Sage Publications.

Kim, Andrew Eungi, and Gil-sung Park. 2003. "Nationalism, Confucianism, Work Ethic and Industrialization in South Korea," *Journal of Contemporary Asia* 33:37–49.

Kim, Claire Jean. 2000. *Bitter Fruit: The Politics of Black-Korean Conflict in New York City*. New Haven, CT: Yale University Press.

Kim, Eleana. 2010. *Adopted Territories: Transnational Adoptees and the Politics of Belonging*. Durham, NC: Duke University Press.

Kim, Jaeeun. 2016. *Contested Embrace: Transborder Membership Politics in Twentieth-Century Korea*. Stanford, CA: Stanford University Press.

Kim, Si Joong. 2003. "The Economic Status and Role of Ethnic Koreans in China," in *The Korean Diaspora in the World Economy*, edited by Inbom Choi and C. Fred Bergsten, 101–30. New York: Columbia University Press.

Kimmel, Michael. 1994. "Masculinity as Homophobia: Fear, Shame, and Silence in the Construction of Gender Identity," in *Theorizing Masculinities*, edited by Harry Brod and Michael Kaufman, 119–42. Thousand Oaks, CA: Sage Publications.

King, Russell, and Anastasia Christou. 2011. "Of Counter-Diaspora and Reverse Transnationalism: Return Mobilities to and from the Ancestral Homeland," *Mobilities* 6:451–66.

King, Russell, Anastasia Christou, and Jill Ahrens. 2011. "'Diverse Mobilities': Second-Generation Greek-Germans Engage with the Homeland as Children and as Adults," *Mobilities* 6:483–501.

Lee, Chae-Jin. 1986. *China's Korean Minority: The Politics of Ethnic Education*. Boulder, CO: Westview Press.

Lee, Stacey J. 2004. "Hmong American Masculinities: Creating New Identities in the United States," in *Adolescent Boys: Exploring Diverse Cultures of Boyhood*, edited by Niobe Way and Judy Y. Chu, 13–30. New York: New York University Press.

Lieberson, Stanley, and Mary C. Waters. 1988. *From Many Strands: Ethnic and Racial Groups in Contemporary America*. New York: Sage Publications.

Lim, Timothy. 2003. "Political Activism and the Expansion of Rights for Transnational Migrant Workers: South Korea and Japan in Comparative Perspective." Working document, Korea and Global Migration Conference, December 11, 2004, Los Angeles.

Louie, Andrea. 2002. "Creating Histories for the Present: Second-Generation (Re)definitions of Chinese American Culture," in *The Changing Face of Home: The Transnational Lives of the Second Generation*, edited by Peggy Levitt and Mary C. Waters, 312–41. New York: Russell Sage Foundation.

Louie, Andrea. 2004. *Chineseness across Borders: Renegotiating Chinese Identities in China and the United States*. Durham, NC: Duke University Press.

Lu, Alexander, and Y. Joel Wong. 2013. "Stressful Experiences of Masculinity among U.S.-Born and Immigrant Asian American Men," *Gender & Society* 27:345.

Mackerras, Colin. 1995. *China's Minority Cultures: Identities and Integration since 1912*. New York: St. Martin's Press.

MacKinnon, Catharine. 1989. *Toward a Feminist Theory of the State*. Cambridge, MA: Harvard University Press.

Masayuki, Suzuki. 1990. "The Korean National Liberation Movement in China and International Response," in *Koreans in China*, edited by Dae-Sook Suh and Edward J. Shultz, 115–43. Honolulu: Center for Korean Studies, University of Hawaii.

Messner, Michael. 1992. *Power at Play: Sports and the Problem of Masculinity*. Boston: Beacon Press.

Min, Pyong Gap. 1992. "A Comparison of the Korean Minorities in China and Japan," *International Migration Review* 26:4–21.

———. 1996. *Caught in the Middle: Korean Communities in New York and Los Angeles*. Berkeley: University of California Press.

———. 2013. "The Immigration of Koreans to the United States," in *Koreans in North America: Their Twenty-First Century Experiences*, edited by Pyong Gap Min. Lanham, MD: Lexington Books.

Min, Pyong Gap, and Chigon Kim. 2013. "Growth and Settlement Patterns of Korean Americans," in *Koreans in North America: Their Twenty-First Century Experiences*, edited by Pyong Gap Min, 35–56. Lanham, MD: Lexington Books.

Moon, Katharine H. S. 2000. "Strangers in the Midst of Globalization: Migrant Workers and Korean Nationalism," in *Korea's Globalization*, edited by Samuel Kim, 147–69. Cambridge: Cambridge University Press.

Nguyen-Akbar, Mytoan. 2014. "The Tensions of Diasporic 'Return' Migration in the Transnational Family," *Journal of Contemporary Ethnography* 43:176–201.

Padavic, Irene, and Barbara Reskin. 1994. *Women and Men at Work.* Thousand Oaks, CA: Pine Forge Press.

Park, Edward J. W., and John S. W. Park. 2005. *Probationary Americans: Contemporary Immigration Policies and the Shaping of Asian American Communities.* New York: Routledge.

Park, Heh-Rahn. 1996. "Narratives of Migration: From the Formation of Korean Chinese Nationality in the PRC to the Emergence of Korean Chinese Migrants in South Korea." Unpublished dissertation, University of Washington, Department of Anthropology.

Park, Jung-Sun, and Paul Y. Chang. 2005. "Contention in the Construction of a Global Korean Community: The Case of the Overseas Korean Act," *Journal of Korean Studies* 10:1–27.

Park, Robert. 1950. *Race and Culture.* Glencoe: Free Press.

Parreñas, Rhacel. 2001. *Servants of Globalization: Women, Migration, and Domestic Work.* Stanford, CA: Stanford University Press.

Piao, Changyu. 1990. "The History of Koreans in China and the Yanbian Korean Autonomous Prefecture," in *Koreans in China,* edited by Dae-Sook Suh and Edward J. Shultz, 44–77. Honolulu: Center for Korean Studies, University of Hawaii.

Pirie, Iain. 2006. "Social Injustice and Economic Dynamism in Contemporary Korea," *Critical Asian Studies* 38:211–43.

Prashad, Vijay. 2000. *The Karma of Brown Folk.* Minneapolis: University of Minnesota Press.

Pyke, Karen, and Denise Johnson. 2003. "Asian American Women and Racialized Femininities: 'Doing' Gender across Cultural Worlds," *Gender & Society* 17:41.

Roberts, Kenneth D. 1997. "China's 'Tidal Wave' of Migrant Labor: What Can We Learn from Mexican Undocumented Migration to the United States?" *International Migration Review* 31(2):249–93.

Romero, Mary. 2002. *Maid in the U.S.A.* London: Routledge.

Roth, Joshua Hotaka. 2002. *Brokered Homeland: Japanese Brazilian Migrants in Japan.* Ithaca, NY: Cornell University Press.

Safran, William. 1988. *Nationalism and Ethnoregional Identities in China*. London: Frank Cass.

Saussure, Ferdinand de. 1916/1974. *Course in General Linguistics*, translated by Wade Baskin. London: Fontana/Collins.

Schmid, Andre. 2002. *Korea between Empires, 1895–1919*. New York: Columbia University Press.

Schwarz, Henry. 1984. *The Minorities of Northern China: A Survey*. Bellingham: Western Washington University.

Seigel, Micol. 2005. "Beyond Compare: Comparative Method after the Transnational Turn," *Radical History Review* 91:62–90.

Seol, Dong-Hoon, and John Skrentny. 2009. "Ethnic Return Migration and Hierarchical Nationhood," *Ethnicities* 9(2):147–74.

Shek, Y. L. 2006. "Asian American Masculinity: A Review of the Literature," *Journal of Men's Studies* 14:379–91.

Shin, Gi-Wook. 2006. *Ethnic Nationalism in Korea: Genealogy, Politics, and Legacy*. Stanford, CA: Stanford University Press.

Shin, Gi-Wook, James Freda, and Gihong Yi. 1999. "The Politics of Ethnic Nationalism in Divided Korea," *Nations and Nationalism* 5(4):469.

Solinger, Dorothy J. 1990. "Citizenship Issues in China's Internal Migration: Comparisons with Germany and Japan," *Political Science Quarterly* 114:455–78.

Tong, Chee-kiong, and Kwok-bun Chan. 2001. "One Face, Many Masks: The Singularity and Plurality of Chinese Identity," *Diaspora* 10:361–89.

Tsuda, Takeyuki. 2003. *Strangers in the Ethnic Homeland*. New York: Columbia University Press.

———. 2016. *Japanese American Ethnicity: In Search of Heritage and Homeland across Generations*. New York: New York University Press.

Tuan, Mia. 2005. *Forever Foreigners or Honorary Whites?: The Asian Ethnic Experience Today*. New Brunswick, NJ: Rutgers University Press.

Umebinyuo, Ijeoma. 2015. "Diaspora Blues," in *Questions for Ada*, edited by Sonya Taaffe and Ijeoma Umebinyuo, 78. CreateSpace Independent Publishing Platform.

Wang, Leslie. 2016. "The Benefits of In-betweenness: Return Migration of Second-generation Chinese American Professionals to China," *Journal of Ethnic and Migration Studies* 42:1941–58.

White, Sydney. 1997. "The Gendered Construction of Naxi Identities," *Modern China* 23:298–327.

Wu, Xiaogang, and Donald Treiman. 2004. "The Household Registration System and Social Stratification in China: 1955–1996," *Demography* 41:363–84.

Yamashiro, Jane H. 2017. *Constructing Japanese American Identity in Japan: Transnationalism, Diaspora, and Ancestral Homeland Migration.* New Brunswick, NJ: Rutgers University Press.

Index

South Korea: comparative wages, 46–47, 49, 60, 62, 128; educational policies, 104; establishment, 18, 105; foreign population, 2, 42; idealized, 114, 123–24; ideologies, 118, 123; immigration policies, 40–42, 47–48, 97, 107, 130, 141; labor movement, 62; language, 104; migration, 8; military, 130; nationalism, 98, 141; parochialism, 121–22; race relations, 8; relations with China, 107; relations with North Korea, 105, 107–8; social activities, 1, 53, 76, 92, 121; social hierarchy, 80; status of men, 77–78; status of women, 74, 81, 84, 87, 91–93; transformation, 8, 87, 118, 121, 125; unemployment and underemployment, 47, 60, 84; worker exploitation, 46, 47, 60, 61–62

South Korean nationalism, 113

South Koreanness, 117, 119

South Koreans: language proficiency, 104, 125; lifestyle, 118–19

standardized exams, 43

Sung Bae, 101–2

talbukja, 105, 165n10. *See also* North Koreans

3-D industries, 44–45, 62, 119

tongil. See Korean reunification

trainee visas, 46, 48

transnationalism, 6–7, 111, 129, 137; future of, 141; historical, 101; logics of, 6

Trump, Donald, 30

Tsolidis, Georgina, 116

Tsuda, Takeyuki, 100, 109

twinkie. *See* FOB–twinkie debate

unassimilable foreigners. *See* perpetual foreigners

undocumented workers, 28, 46, 62, 97

United States: Asian stereotypes, 71–72, 79–80, 139–40; educational policies, 31; gender ideologies, 83, 84, 86–87; idealized, 86–87; immigration policies, 30; Korean immigration, 18–20, 21; military, 19, 108; status of women, 87; workplace culture, 55, 86

unskilled work. *See* manual work

upward mobility. *See* economic mobility

Veronica, 92, 93

visas, 39–40, 42, 44, 46, 65. *See also* individual visa categories

War Brides Act, 19

Waters, Mary, 32–33

Westernization, 89, 123–24

White Americans, 51, 56, 66, 79, 85, 95, 127

white-collar work. *See* professional work

whiteness, 29–30, 31–33, 57, 139; as "real" Americanness, 26, 36, 64, 140, 158

white privilege, 78

Wong, Y. Joel, 72

workplace culture, 53–56, 58; ethics, 54–55; gender roles, 53–54, 84–85; hierarchy, 53; social functions, 53–54

World War II, 19

Xi, Xiaoxing, 140

Yamashiro, Jane, 112–13

Yanbian Korean Autonomous Prefecture, 18, 22, 26–29, 45, 105, 113, 122, 128

Yellow Peril, 71

Yeongdeungpo-gu, 110

Yongsan-gu, 166n15

Yu Na, 45, 48, 61, 111

About the Author

HELENE K. LEE received her PhD in Sociology from the University of California, Santa Barbara, and is currently an assistant professor in the Department of Sociology at Dickinson College.

CPSIA information can be obtained
at www.ICGtesting.com
Printed in the USA
LVOW08*2303221217
560487LV00002B/6/P